German Phrase Book

The Ultimate German Phrase Book for Travelers of Germany, Including Over 1000 Phrases for Accommodations, Eating, Traveling, Shopping, and More

© **Copyright 2018**

All rights Reserved. No part of this book may be reproduced in any form without permission in writing from the author. Reviewers may quote brief passages in reviews.

Disclaimer: No part of this publication may be reproduced or transmitted in any form or by any means, mechanical or electronic, including photocopying or recording, or by any information storage and retrieval system, or transmitted by email without permission in writing from the publisher.

While all attempts have been made to verify the information provided in this publication, neither the author nor the publisher assumes any responsibility for errors, omissions or contrary interpretations of the subject matter herein.

This book is for entertainment purposes only. The views expressed are those of the author alone, and should not be taken as expert instruction or commands. The reader is responsible for his or her own actions.

Adherence to all applicable laws and regulations, including international, federal, state and local laws governing professional licensing, business practices, advertising and all other aspects of doing business in the US, Canada, UK or any other jurisdiction is the sole responsibility of the purchaser or reader.

Neither the author nor the publisher assumes any responsibility or liability whatsoever on the behalf of the purchaser or reader of these materials. Any perceived slight of any individual or organization is purely unintentional.

Contents

INTRODUCTION 1

CHAPTER 1 – PRONUNCIATION 3

CHAPTER 2 – STANDARD PHRASES IN GERMAN 7
- Everyday words 7
- Understanding 8
- Signs 8
- Greeting 9
- Saying "Bye" 9
- To apologize to someone / Thank someone 9
- Compliments 10
- How are you? 10
- Asking for opinions and expressing yourself 11
- Religion 12
- Traveling by public transport 13
- Getting to know each other 13
- Make an appointment 13
- Cursing 14
- Being upset with something/someone 14
- Events and activities 14

CHAPTER 3 – NUMBERS AND COLORS 17
- Time 18
- Time of the day 19
- Duration 19
- Days 20
- Months 20
- Colors 20

CHAPTER 4 – TRANSPORT 22
- Passport control and customs 22
- Bus and Train 23
- Direction 26
- Taxi 27
- Boat 28

CHAPTER 5 – ACCOMMODATION 33
- Finding accommodation 33
- Reservation 33
- Camping 36
- Complaints 36

CHAPTER 6 – MONEY 40

CHAPTER 7 – RESTAURANTS AND FOOD 41
Reservation and Ordering 41
Ordering snacks 43

CHAPTER 8 – BARS 47
Ordering drinks 47
Asking for internet and WiFi 49
The day after 49
Smoking 50

CHAPTER 9 – SHOPPING 54
Making a decision 55
Finding products 56
At a hair salon 57

CHAPTER 10 – DRIVING 61

CHAPTER 11 – AUTHORITIES 69

CHAPTER 12 – EMERGENCIES 70
Health 71
At the pharmacy 71
Visiting a doctor 73

CHAPTER 13 - SERVICES AND REPAIRS 86
Photography 87
Post office 88
Bank 89
ATM 92

CHAPTER 14 – SPARE TIME 96
Teathre 96
The club 97
Flirting – Small Talk 98
Museum and Gallery 100

CHAPTER 15 – USEFUL WORDS AND TERMS 106

CHAPTER 16 – TIPS FOR LEARNING A NEW LANGUAGE 123

CHAPTER 17 – BONUS – WRITING AN E-MAIL 128

CONCLUSION 131

Introduction

The phrases "Ein Bier bitte" (One beer, please) and "Wo ist die Toilette?" (Where is the toilet?) are always good to know. It is definitely enough for a night in a German club. But for a whole journey through Germany, you need a lot more than that.

Have you ever been embarrassed to travel to a country without knowing a word in the local language? A whole new dimension of experiences, on the other hand, opens up for the traveler, when he can talk to the locals in their language! Although most Germans know at least a few words in a foreign language - mostly English, French or Spanish - they would definitely appreciate it if you knew some of the most important phrases in German. Learning languages is certainly not easy, but doable! And we're not talking about learning foreign languages to perfection. Isn't it frustrating, even depressing, when you can not talk to other people on a trip and have to spend every evening alone? And is it even exciting if you can not communicate with the locals? Consider how much interesting information and enriching contacts you are missing! Also, when you know some of the phrases, it's much less stressful and uncomplicated to reserve a hotel, tell the pharmacist about your headache, and order your food. Especially since there are many travel destinations and regions where people don't understand a word in English. And your hands and feet are not always enough for communication.

We have collected the most helpful sentences and phrases that are useful in all possible situations you may find yourself in. It always makes sense to know the most important phrases in the language of your travel destination. By that we mean that you can say who you are, where you come from, and you can ask for the way or the time.

In this book, you'll find over 1000 phrases in German with English translations, from greetings and directions to restaurants, shopping and night-life. Don't worry - we made sure that the phrases are simple and easy to understand. Also, you'll learn how to pronounce some letter combinations and words. One thing is sure, you'll definitely be able to communicate with people. Everything you need is right in front of you. This is the solution to your communication problems when you travel to Germany. You can get the phrase you need by using the table of contents that will lead you to the topic you are looking for: bank, bar, shopping, transport, restaurant, and many others. With all this being said, you can pack your bags and enjoy your trip to Germany!

Chapter 1 – Pronunciation

In the German language, pronunciation is one of the things you get better at with time. However, some rules can help you to read unfamiliar words correctly.

The German alphabet has 26 letters of the Latin alphabet plus the special characters ä, ö, ü and ß. But there are also German sounds, which are not represented by a separate, individual character, but by a combination of characters.

These are the consonants:

- ch
- ng
- sch

and the diphthongs:

- au
- ei
- eu / äu

sch is being pronounced as the English "sh" e.g. in short.

ng stands for a nasal and it's the closest to the "n" in enl. "singer." You do not hear a g!

äu and **eu** are pronounced the same. Äu is written when the word is closely related to a word with au, such as "Häute", the plural of Haut (skin). In all other cases, eu is written.

The diphtongs are composed of two vowels, but they are so close together that they make one sound.

ch is being pronounced like:

[x] after a, o, u and au (Bach, doch, Buch, auch)

[ç] after all other vowels, after l, n and r and in the endings -chen and -ig (Bäche, ich, Bücher, echt, Milch, durch, manchmal, Mädchen, einig)

[k] before a, o, u, l, r and s (Chaos, Chor, Chlor, sechs)

The pronunciation of ch can in Singular be different than in the plural! Example: das Buch ([X]), die Bücher ([ç]).

h is pronounced when at the beginning of the word and syllable.

If **h** is an elongation sign, its not being pronounced. [h]: Hund, Hunde | hütte, unter|halten; **h** (mute), long vowel: Drohung, sehen, gehen, ruh

st / sp - at the beginning of the word and syllable st is pronounced as "scht" and sp as "schp". (Stein, ver|stecken, Sprache, aus|sprechen, aber Ast [st], Wes|pe [sp] etc.)

b, d, g, s, v - at the word and syllable end b, d, g, s and v are pronounced as [p], [t], [k], [s] and [f]. (ab [p], und [t], Weg|gang [k], Haus|tür [s], positiv [f]).

Length and shortness of vowels

The two English words *shit* and *sheet* differ in pronunciation only by the vowel. Shit is short, sheet long. In the German language, there is a long and a short form of all vowels.

It is important to clearly show the difference between long/short in the accented syllables.

Length can be signaled by the following means:

Doubling the vowel at a, e, and o, e.g. in Saal (hall), See (lake) and Boot (boat).

h as an elongation sign possible after all vowels. The h is then not spoken, but only indicates the length of the vocal. (For example, Ahle (awl), sehen(see), ihr(her), ohne(without), Uhr(watch), nähen(sew), Bühne(stage), Höhe(height).

Long **i** is written as **ie** or in exceptional cases as **ieh** (ziehen(pull), Vieh (cattle), etc.). The e (and the h) are not spoken in this combination, but indicate the length of the i such as in Miete(rent), lieben(love) oder die(the).

These length signs are always correct; that means that these vowels are always long. Unfortunately, not all long vowels are explicitly marked. The a in the Tal(valley) or the o in the Rose(rose) are also long. The spelling offers no direct help here.

But there is a strict rule:

Often (but not always) the vowel is spoken long, if only one root consonant follows it.

Examples:

a in Tag(day)

e in Leben(life): [e:]

ö in stör-t(trouble)

ü in üb-t (practice)

Shortness is signaled by the doubling of the following consonant.

The following vowels are all short:

a in Stall (stable)

e in den(because): [ε]

i in Mitte(middle)

o in kommen(come)

u in Tunnel(tunnel)

Not all short vowels are marked as such by doubling the following consonant. However, double consonants always show shortness, except for s, for example, the word Fuß(foot) is pronounced with long u.

In German after a long vowel and diphthong, ß (Eszett) is written. The Eszett indicates that the previous vowel is long.

often (but not always) short, if followed by several consonants.

For example:

a in Last(burden)

e in Herbst (autumn)

i in Tinte(ink)

Chapter 2 – Standard phrases in German

Here is a list of the most important standard phrases of the German language. These are the standard phrases that are being used frequently. We have some everyday words for you as well as phrases you can use when you make small-talk with a stranger or a friend. Basic phrases like "hello, please, thank you," and "goodbye" should be very helpful at the beginning. The list is helpful for both beginners and advanced.

Everyday words

Ja - Yes

Nein - No

Bitte - Please

Danke – Thank you

Entschuldigung – Excuse me

Wie bitte? - Pardon?

Es tut mir leid. - I'm sorry (apologizing for something)

Wo? - Where?

Warum? - Why?

Wann? - When?

Wer? - Who?

Wie? - How?

Hier - Here

Dort – There

Understanding

Ich verstehe. - I understand.

Ich verstehe nicht. – I don't understand.

Bitte sprechen Sie langsam. – Please speak slowly.

Können Sie das bitte wiederholen? – Could you repeat that, please?

Können Sie das bitte aufschreiben? - Could you write that down, please?

Sprechen Sie Englisch? - Do you speak English?

Sprechen Sie Französisch? – Do you speak French?

Sprechen Sie Deutsch? – Do you speak German?

Sprechen Sie Spanisch? – Do you speak Spanish?

Sprechen Sie Italienisch? - Do you speak Italian?

Signs

Geöffnet – open

Geschlossen - closed

Eingang - entrance

Ausgang - exit

Drücken - push

Ziehen - pull

Männer – men

Damen - women

Besetzt - occupied

Frei – vacant

Greeting

-Wie geht's dir? / Wie geht es Ihnen? (formal speech) – Gut. / Ganz gut. / Nicht so gut.

(How are you? / How are you? - Good. / Quite well. / Not so good.)

-Hallo. / Guten Morgen / Guten Tag / Guten Abend

(Hello. / Good morning / Good day / Good evening)

-Tschüss. / Auf Wiedersehen.

(Bye / Goodbye)

-Wie heißt du? – Ich heiße…

(What is your name? - My name is…)

-Woher kommst du? – Ich komme aus…

(Where are you from? - I'm from…)

Saying "Bye"

-Tschüss/ Auf Wiedersehen (formal speech), schönen Tag noch.

(Bye/ Until we meet again, have a nice day.)

-Schönes Wochenende.

(nice weekend)

-Mach's gut. Antwort: Mach's besser. / Du auch.

(Take care. Answer: You too)

-Man sieht sich.

(See you)

- Ciao. (= „Tschau")

 (Ciao)

To apologize to someone / Thank someone

-Entschuldigung.

(Sorry)

-Tut mir leid.

(I am sorry)

-Danke. Vielen Dank.

(Thanks. Thank you very much)

-Gerne. / Gern geschehen. / Keine Ursache.

(Gladly./ You are welcome. /Never mind.)

-Schon gut.

(It's fine.)

Compliments

-Das sieht aber gut aus.

(That looks good.)

-Du bist sehr sympathisch.

(You are very sympathetic.)

-Du siehst wirklich toll aus.

(You look really good.)

-Gute Arbeit!

(Good job!)

-Gut gemacht!

(Well done!)

How are you?

-Wie geht es dir / Ihnen?

(How are you / you?)

-Mir geht's gut.

(I'm fine.)

-Gut und selbst?

(Good and you?)

-Hast du dich in deiner neuen Wohnung gut eingelebt?

(Have you settled in well in your new apartment?)

-Ich fühle mich nicht wohl. (krank)

(I am not feeling well. (Sick))

Asking for opinions and expressing yourself

was meinst du? - what do you think?

ich finde, dass ... - I think that ...

ich hoffe, dass ... - I hope that ...

ich fürchte, dass ... - I'm afraid that ...

meiner Meinung nach ... - in my opinion, ...

ich bin einverstanden - I agree

ich bin nicht einverstanden - I disagree or I don't agree

das ist wahr - that's true

das ist nicht wahr - that's not true

Ich denke schon - I think so

Ich denke nicht - I don't think so

Ich hoffe es - I hope so

Ich hoffe nicht - I hope not

du hast Recht - you're right

du liegst falsch - you're wrong

es macht mir nichts aus - I don't mind

das hängt von dir ab - it's up to you

es kommt darauf an - that depends

das ist interessant - that's interesting

das ist lustig - that's funny

Religion

Bist du religiös? - Are you religious?

Nein, ich bin ... - No, I'm ...

Atheist - an atheist

Agnostiker - agnostic

Welcher Konfession gehörst du an? - What religion are you?

Ich bin ... - I'm a ...

Christ - Christian

Muslim - Muslim

Buddhist - Buddhist

Sikh - Sikh

Hindu - Hindu

Protestant - Protestant

Katholik - Catholic

ich bin Jude - I'm Jewish

Glaubst du an Gott? - Do you believe in God?

Ich glaube an Gott - I believe in God

Ich glaube nicht an Gott - I don't believe in God

Glaubst du an ein Leben nach dem Tod? - Do you believe in life after death?

Glaubst du an Wiedergeburt? - Do you believe in reincarnation?

Gibts es ... in der Nähe? - is there a ... nearby?

eine Kirche - church

eine Moschee - mosque

eine Synagoge - synagogue

einen Tempel - temple

Traveling by public transport

-Wann fährt die nächste Bahn Richtung Hauptbahnhof?

(When is the next train to the main station?)

-Welches Ticket / welche Preisstufe brauche ich bis [Haltestelle]?

(Which ticket / price level do I need until [stop]?)

-Von welchem Gleis fährt…?

(From which track ...?)

-Der Zug hat 10 Minuten Verspätung.

(The train is 10 minutes late.)

- Ist dieser Platz noch frei?

(Is this seat free?)

Getting to know each other

-Wie heißt du? – Ich heiße…

(What is your name? - My name is…)

-Woher kommst du? – Ich komme aus…

(Where are you from? - I'm from…)

-Was machst du beruflich? – Ich bin…

(What are you doing professionally? - I am…)

-Seit wann bist du in Deutschland?

(Since when are you in Germany?)

- Kennst du …?

(Do you know ...?)

Make an appointment

-Hast du Lust, morgen ins Kino zu gehen?

(Do you want to go to the cinema tomorrow?)

-Lass uns morgen ins Kino gehen.

(Let's go to the cinema tomorrow.)

-Wann treffen wir uns?

(When/At what time are we meeting?)

-Hast du morgen Zeit?

(Do you have time tomorrow?)

-Lass uns nochmal telefonieren…

(Let's talk again (on the phone) …)

Cursing

-So ein Mist!

(Crap!)

-Och nö! / Oh nein! (First one is slang)

(Oh no!)

-Das darf doch wohl nicht wahr sein!

(This can't be happening!)

Being upset with something/someone

-Das soll wohl doch ein Witz sein?

(That's supposed to be a joke?)

-Spinnst du?

(Are you crazy?)

-Du bist wohl verrückt geworden!

(You must have gone crazy!)

- Das ist eine Unverschämtheit!

(That's an impudence!)

Events and activities

Was interessiert Sie (denn) besonders? - What are you interested in?

Gibt es zur Zeit irgendwelche …? - Are there any … on at the moment?

Ausstellungen - exhibitions

kulturellen Veranstaltungen - cultural events

Sportveranstaltungen - sporting events

Gibt es hier irgendwelche …? - Are there any …?

Ausflüge - excursions

Touren - tours

Tagestouren - day trips

Gibt es hier eine Stadtrundfahrt? - Is there a city tour?

Können Sie uns sagen, was zur Zeit … läuft? - Could you tell us what's on at the …?

im Kino - cinema

im Theater - theatre

in der Konzerthalle - concert hall

in der Oper - opera house

Kann ich hier Karten reservieren? - Can I book tickets here?

Haben Sie Broschüren über/von …? - Do you have any brochures on …?

lokalen Sehenswürdigkeiten - local attractions

Können Sie ein gutes Restaurant empfehlen? - Can you recommend a good restaurant?

Haben Sie… - Do you have a map of the…

einen Stadtplan - city

einen Stadtplan - town

Wo ist …? - Where's the …?

das Stadtzentrum? - city centre

die Kunstgalerie? - art gallery

das Museum? - museum

die Einkaufsstraße - main shopping street

der Markt - market

der Bahnhof - railway station

Womit kommt man am besten in der Stadt herum? - What's the best way of getting around the city?

Wo kann ich ein Auto mieten? - Where can I rent a car?

Chapter 3 – Numbers and Colors

Numbers are everywhere and they are important because of many reasons. When you find yourself somewhere and need to know the time or if you need to tell someone how much something costs, than you will certainly find it helpful.

eins >> one

zwei >> two

drei >> three

vier >> four

fünf >> five

sechs >> six

sieben >> seven

acht >> eight

neun >> nine

zehn >> ten

elf >> eleven

zwölf >> twelve

dreizehn >> thirteen

vierzehn >> fourteen

fünfzehn >> fifteen

sechszehn >> sixteen

seibzehn>> seventeen

achtzehn >> eighteen

neunzehn >> nineteen

zwanzig >> twenty

einundzwanzig>> twenty one

zweiundzwanzig>> twenty two

dreiundzwanzig >> twenty three

dreißig >> thirty

vierzig>> forty

fünfzig >> fifty

sechzig >> sixty

siebzig >> seventy

achtzig >> eighty

neunzig >> ninety

hundert >> one hundred

zweihundert >> two hundred

dreihundert >> three hundred

tausend >> one thousand

zweitausend >> two thousand

eine Million>> one million

eine Billion >> one billion

eine Hälfte >> half

weniger >> less

mehr >> more

Time

jetzt >> now

später >> later

vorher >> before

Morgen >> morning

Nachmittag >> afternoon

Abend>> evening

Nacht >> night

Heute >> today

Gestern >> yesterday

morgen>> tomorrow

diese Woche >> this week

letzte Woche >> last week

nächste Woche >> next week

Time of the day

ein Uhr >> one o'clock AM

zwei Uhr >> two o'clock AM

Mittag >> noon

dreizehn Uhr >> one o'clock PM

vierzehn Uhr >> two o'clock PM

Mitternacht >> midnight

halb eun >> half past eight - häufig auch nur: half eight

Duration

_____ Minute >> _____ minute

_____ Stunde >> _____ hour

_____ Tag >> _____ day

_____ Woche >> _____ week

_____ Monat >> _____ month

_____ Jahr >> _____ year

Days

Sonntag >> Sunday

Montag >> Monday

Dienstag >> Tuesday

Mittwoch >> Wednesday

Donnerstag >> Thursday

Freitag >> Friday

Samstag >> Saturday

Months

Januar >> January

Februar >> February

März >> March

April >> April

Mai >> May

Juni >> June

Juli >> July

August >> August

September >> September

Oktober >> October

November >> November

Dezember >> December

Colors

schwarz >> black

weiss >> white

grau >> grey

rot >> red

blau >> blue

gelb >> yellow

grün >> green

orange >> orange

lila >> purple

braun >> brown

Chapter 4 – Transport

The streets can be complicated sometimes and with all the cars, buses and trains, one gets lost easily. You will probably use public transport to travel, such as the train, subway or bus . Or you may go for a walk and need help reaching your destination. Either way, you should remember a few simple questions to ask for directions, buy tickets, or find your way around. If you can tell people where you want to go, you should find your way with a little luck. Even if you do not understand otherwise, these phrases will help you direct your taxi drivers and get rudimentary advice from people on the street. Here are some of the most important phrases to get you to your destination as soon as possible.

Passport control and customs

Darf ich bitte Ihren Pass sehen? - Could I see your passport, please?

Woher reisen Sie ein? - Where have you travelled from?

Was ist der Grund Ihrer Einreise? - What's the purpose of your visit?

Ich bin auf Urlaub - I'm on holiday.

Ich bin auf Geschäftsreise - I'm on business.

Ich besuche Verwandte - I'm visiting relatives.

Wie lange werden Sie sich im Lande aufhalten? - How long will you be staying?

Wo werden Sie übernachten? - Where will you be staying?

Sie müssen … ausfüllen - You have to fill in this …

diese Einreisekarte - landing card

dieses Einreiseformular - immigration form

Genießen Sie ihren Aufenthalt - Enjoy your stay!

Würden Sie bitte Ihre Tasche aufmachen? - Could you open your bag, please?

Haben Sie etwas zu verzollen? - Do you have anything to declare?

Diese Waren sind zollpflichtig - You have to pay duty on these items.

Bus and Train

Wieviel kostet ein Ticket nach _____? - How much is a ticket to _____?

Eine Fahrkarte nach _____, bitte. - One ticket to _____, please.

Wohin geht dieser Zug/ Bus? - Where does this train/ bus go?

Wo ist der Zug/ Bus nach _____? - Where is the train/ bus to _____?

Hält dieser Zug/ Bus in _____? - Does this train/ bus stop in _____?

Wann fährt der Zug/ Bus nach_____ ? - When does the train/ bus for _____ leave?

Wann wird dieser Zug/ Bus in _____ ankommen? - When will this train/ bus arrive in _____?

Wo befindet sich der Fahrkartenschalter? - Where's the ticket office?

Wo befinden sich die Fahrkartenautomaten? - Where are the ticket machines?

Wann fährt der nächste Bus …? - What time's the next bus to …?

Wann fährt der nächste Zug nach …? - What time's the next train to …?

Kann ich den Fahrschein im Bus kaufen? - Can I buy a ticket on the bus?

Kann ich den Fahrschein im Zug kaufen? - Can I buy a ticket on the train?

Was kostet … nach Frankfurt? - How much is a … to Frankfurt?

Eine einfache Fahrt - Single

Ein Hin- und Rückfahrticket - Return

Eine einfache Fahrt erster Klasse - First class single

Ein Hin- und Rückfahrticket erster Klasse - First class return

Einen Einzelfahrschein für Kinder - Child single

Einen Hin- und Rückfahrschein für Kinder - Child return

Einen Einzelfahrschein für Senioren – Senior citizens' single

Einen Hin- und Rückfahrschein für Senioren - Senior citizens' return

Ist das Ticket außerhalb der Stoßzeiten billiger? - Are there any reductions for off-peak travel?

Wann möchten Sie fahren? - When would you like to travel?

Wann möchten Sie zurückfahren? - When will you be coming back?

Ich hätte gerne einen Hin- und Rückfahrschein nach … , mit Rückfahrt am Sonntag - I'd like a return to …, coming back on Sunday

Welchen Bahnsteig brauche ich für …? - Which platform do I need for …?

Ist dies der richtige Gleis nach …? - Is this the right platform for …?

Wo muss ich nach … umsteigen? - Where do I change for …?

Sie müssen in … umsteigen - You'll need to change at …

Kann ich bitte einen Fahrplan haben? - Can I have a timetable, please?

Wie oft fahren die Busse …? - How often do the buses run to …?

Wie oft fahren die Züge …? - How often do the trains run to …?

Ich möchte gern meinen Saisonfahrschein erneuern - I'd like to renew my season ticket, please.

Der Zug hat Verspätung - The train's running late.

Der Zug wurde gestrichen - The train's been cancelled.

Hält dieser Bus …? - Does this bus stop at …?

Hält dieser Zug …? - Does this train stop at …?

Könnten Sie das in den Laderaum legen, bitte? - Could I put this in the hold, please?

Könnten Sie mir sagen, wann wir ... ankommen? - Could you tell me when we get to ...?

Könnten Sie bitte ... anhalten? - Could you please stop at ...?

Macht es Ihnen etwas aus, wenn ich mich hier hinsetze? - Do you mind if I sit here?

Die Fahrscheine bitte - Tickets, please.

Alle Fahrscheine und Bahnkarten bitte - All tickets and railcards, please.

Darf ich bitte Ihren Fahrschein sehen? - Could I see your ticket, please?

Ich habe meinen Fahrschein verloren - I've lost my ticket.

Wann kommen wir in ... an? - What time do we arrive in ...?

Welche Haltestelle ist das hier? - What's this stop?

Welche ist die nächste Haltstelle? - What's the next stop?

Das ist meine Haltestelle - This is my stop.

Ich steige hier aus - I'm getting off here.

Gibt es einen Speisewagen im Zug? - Is there a buffet car on the train?

Stört es Sie, wenn ich das Fenster aufmache? - Do you mind if I open the window?

Dieser Zug endet hier - This train terminates here.

Alle Passagiere bitte aussteigen! - All change, please.

Vergessen Sie bitte nicht Ihr Gepäck - Please take all your luggage and personal belongings with you.

Wieviele Haltestellen sind es bis ... - How many stops is it to ...?

Ich möchte bitte eine Tageskarte - I'd like a Day Travelcard, please.

Für welche Zonen? - Which zones?

Direction

Wie komme ich zu _____ ? How do I get to _____ ?

...zum Bahnhof? ...the train station?

...zur Bushaltestelle? ...the bus station?

...zum Flughafen? ...the airport?

...zum Stadtzentrum? ...downtown?

...zur Jugendherberge? ...the hostel?

...zum _____ Hotel? ...the _____ hotel?

...zur amerikanischen/ kanadischen/ australischen/ britischenBotschaft? ...the American/ Canadian/ Australian/ British consulate?

...zur deutschen/ österreichischen/ schweizer Botschaft? ...the German/ Austrian/ Swiss consulate?

Wo gibt es viele... Where are there a lot of...

...Hotels? ...hotels?

...Restaurants? ...restaurants?

...Bars? ...bars?

...Sehenswürdigkeiten? ...sights to see?

Könnten Sie es mir auf der Karte zeigen? Can you show me on the map?

Straße - street

Nach links drehen/ abbiegen. - Turn left.

Nach rechts drehen/ abbiegen. - Turn right.

links - left

rechts - right

geradeaus - straight ahead

folgen _____ - towards the _____

nach der _____ - past the _____

vor der _____ - before the _____

Nach _____ schauen. - Watch for the _____.

Norden - north

Süden - south

Osten - east

Westen - west

oberhalb – uphill/above

unterhalb – downhill/below

Taxi

Taxi! - Taxi!

Fahren Sie mich bitte nach _____. - Take me to _____, please.

Wieviel kostet es nach _____ zu fahren? - How much does it cost to get to _____?

Bringen Sie mich bitte dort hin.- Take me there, please.

Wie lange dauert es bis dahin? - How long will the journey take?

Stört es Sie, wenn ich das Fenster aufmache? - Do you mind if I open the window?

Stört es Sie, wenn ich das Fenster zumache? - Do you mind if I close the window?

Sind wir bald da? - Are we almost there?

Wieviel kostet das? - How much is it?

Haben Sie es ein bisschen kleiner? - Have you got this in a smaller size?

Danke, der Rest ist für Sie - That's fine, keep the change.

Möchten Sie eine Rechnung/ einen Beleg? - Would you like a receipt?

Kann ich bitte einen Beleghaben? - Could I have a receipt, please?

Können Sie mich hier um … abholen? - Could you pick me up here at … (time)?

Können Sie hier auf mich warten? - Could you wait for me here?

Wo sind Sie? – Where are you?

Wie lautet die Adresse? - What's the address?

Ich bin ... - I'm ...

im Metropolitan Hotel - at the Metropolitan Hotel

am Bahnhof - at the train station

Wie lautet Ihr Name, bitte? - Could I take your name, please?

Wie lange muss ich warten? - How long will I have to wait?

Wie lange dauert es? - How long will it be?

Es ist auf dem Weg - It's on its way.

Wohin möchten Sie? - Where would you like to go?

Ich möchte ... - I'd like to go to ...

zum Bahnhof – to the train station

Können Sie mich ... bringen - Could you take me to ...?

zum Stadtzentrum - the city centre

Wie viel würde es ... kosten? - How much would it cost to ...?

zum Flughafen – the airport

Könnten wir an einem Bankautomat anhalten? - Could we stop at a cashpoint?

Ist das Taximeter eingeschaltet? - Is the meter switched on?

Bitte schalten Sie das Taximeter ein - Please switch the meter on.

Boat

Wann fährt das nächste Schiff nach ...? - What time's the next boat to ...?

Ich möchte bitte eine ...Kabine - I'd like a ... cabin

Zweier-Kabine - two-berth

Vierer-Kabine - four-berth

Wir brauchen keine Kabine - We don't need a cabin

Ich möchte bitte ein Ticket für ein Auto und zwei Passagiere - I'd like a ticket for a car and two passengers.

Ich möchte bitte ein Fußgängerticket - I'd like a ticket for a foot passenger.

Wie lange dauert die Überfahrt? - How long does the crossing take?

Wann kommt die Fähre in … an? - What time does the ferry arrive in …?

Wie lange müssen wir vor der Abfahrt da sein? - How soon before the departure time do we have to arrive?

Wo ist der Informationsschalter? - Where's the information desk?

Wo ist die Kabinennummer …? - Where's cabin number …?

Auf welchem Deck ist/befindet sich …? - Which deck's the … on?

das Büffet - buffet

das Restaurant - restaurant

die Bar - bar

der Laden - shop

das Kino – cinema

Ich bin seekrank - I feel seasick.

Der See ist sehr rau - The sea's very rough.

Der See ist ziemlich ruhig - The sea's quite calm.

Wir bitten alle Autofahrer, sich zu ihrem Fahrzeug zu begeben, um von Bord zu gehen - All car passengers, please make your way down to the car decks for disembarkation.

Wir werden unseren Zielhafen in ungefähr 30 Minuten erreichen - We will be arriving in port in approximately 30 minutes' time.

Könnten Sie bitte Ihre Kabinen räumen? - Please vacate your cabins.

Important terms

Timetable - Fahrplan

single -Einzelfahrschein
return -Rückfahrt
platform - Bahnsteig, Bussteig
waiting room - Wartesaal
ticket office - Fahrkartenschalter
seat - Sitz
seat number - Sitznummer
luggage rack - Gepäckablage
first class - erste Klasse
second class - zweite Klasse
ticket inspector - Schaffner, Schaffnerin
ticket collector - Fahrkartenkontrolleur, Fahrkartenkontrolleurin
penalty fare - erhöhtes Beförderungsentgelt
buffet car - Speisewagen
carriage - Waggon
compartment - Abteil
derailment - Entgleisen
express train - Schnellzug
guard - Schaffner, Schaffnerin
level crossing - Bahnübergang
line closure - Streckensperrung
live rail - Stromschiene
railcard - Bahncard
railway line - Bahntrasse
restaurant car - Speisewagen
season ticket - Zeitkarte
signal - Signal

sleeper train - Schlafwagon
station - Bahnhof
railway station - Bahnhof
train station - Bahnhof
stopping service - Eilzug
ticket barrier - Sperre zur Fahrkartenkontrolle
track - Strecke
train - Zug
train crash - Zugunglück
train driver - Zugführer
train fare - Fahrpreis
train journey - Zugreise
travelcard - Mehrfahrtenkarte
Tube station or underground station - U-Bahn-Haltestelle
Tunnel - Tunnel
bus driver - Busfahrer, Busfahrerin
bus fare - Fahrpreis
bus journey - Busreise
bus stop - Bushaltestelle
bus lane - Busspur
bus station - Busbahnhof
conductor - Fahrtbegleiter, Fahrtbegleiterin
inspector - Aufseher, Aufseherin
luggage hold - Gepäckraum
the next stop - nächste Haltestelle
night bus - Nachtbus
request stop - Bedarfshaltestelle

route - Strecke

terminus - Endstation

Chapter 5 – Accommodation

When you arrive to your destination, you need to get into your accommodations. Do you want to book a room, ask for breakfast, or report to the front desk that you have lost your key? Do not worry! Learn only a few words and have the courage to use them, too, and you will be able to quickly understand! These simple phrases will help you out.

Finding accommodation

Wir suchen nach einer Unterkunft - We're looking for accommodation.

Wir brauchen eine Unterkunft - We need somewhere to stay.

Haben Sie eine Liste mit/von …? - Do you have a list of …?

Hotels - Hotels

Pensionen - B&Bs (bed and breakfasts)

Jugendherbergen - youth hostels

Campingplätzen - campsites

Was für eine Art Unterkunft suchen Sie? - What sort of accommodation are you looking for?

Können Sie eine Unterkunft für mich buchen? - Can you book accommodation for me?

Reservation

Darf ich bitte Ihren Pass sehen? - Could I see your passport?

Würden Sie bitte dieses Anmeldeformular ausfüllen? - Could you please fill in this registration form?

Haben Sie ein freies Zimmer? - Do you have any rooms available?

Wie viel kostet ein Zimmer für eine Person/zwei Personen? - How much is a room for one person/two people?

Gibt es im Zimmer... - Does the room come with...

...ein Badezimmer? ...a bathroom?

...ein Telefon? ...a telephone?

...ein TV? ...a TV?

Kann ich das Zimmer zuerst besichtigen? - May I see the room first?

Haben Sie etwas ruhigeres? - Do you have anything quieter?

...kleineres?...smaller?

...grösseres? ...bigger?

...saubereres? ...cleaner?

...billigeres? ...cheaper?

OK, ich nehme es. - OK, I'll take it.

Ich will _____ Nacht/Nächte bleiben. - I will stay for _____ night.

Können Sie mir ein anderes Hotel empfehlen? - Can you suggest another hotel?

Haben Sie einen Safe? - Do you have a safe?

...Schliessfächer? - ...lockers?

Ist das Frühstück/Abendessen inklusive? - Is breakfast/supper included?

Um welche Zeit ist das Frühstück/Abendessen? - What time is breakfast/supper?

Kann ich das Frühstück bitte aufs Zimmer haben? - Could I have breakfast in my room, please?

Wann schließt die Bar?- What time does the bar close?

Brauchen Sie Hilfe mit Ihrem Gepäck? - Would you like any help with your luggage?

Bitte reinigen Sie mein Zimmer. - Please clean my room.

Können Sie mich um ____wecken? - Can you wake me at ____?

Ich möchte mich abmelden. - I want to check out.

Wo ist der Aufzug? - Where are the elevators?

Ich glaube, in der Rechnung steckt ein Fehler - I think there's a mistake in this bill.

Wie möchten Sie bezahlen? - How would you like to pay?

Ich zahle … - I'll pay …

per Kreditkarte - by credit card

bar - in cash

Haben Sie die Minibar benutzt? - Have you used the minibar?

Wir haben die Minibar nicht benutzt - We haven't used the minibar.

Kann uns jemand beim Transport des Gepäcks behilflich sein? - Could we have some help bringing our luggage down?

Können wir unser Gepäck hier irgendwo aufbewahren? - Do you have anywhere we could leave our luggage?

Kann ich bitte eine Rechnung/ einen Beleg haben? - Could I have a receipt, please?

Würden Sie mir bitte ein Taxi rufen? - Could you please call me a taxi?

Ich hoffe, Sie hatten einen angenehmen Aufenthalt - I hope you had an enjoyable stay.

Ich habe meinen Aufenthalt hier sehr genossen - I've really enjoyed my stay.

Wir haben unseren Aufenthalt hier sehr genossen - We've really enjoyed our stay.

Camping

Der Campingplatz - Campsite

Das Zelt - Tent

Der Wohnwagen - Caravan

Das Wohnmobil – Motor home

Haben Sie freie Stellplätze? – Do you have any pitches free?

Kann ich neben meinem Stellplatz parken? – Can I park beside the pitch?

Stellplatz mit Stromanschluß – Serviced pitch

Stellplatz ohne Stromanschluß - Unserviced pitch

Stromanschluß – Electrical connection

Wieviel kostet eine Übernachtung? – What is the charge per night?

Wo sind die Duschen? Where are the showers?

Wo kann man Wäsche waschen? – Where are the laundry facilities?

Ist das Trinkwasser? Is this drinking water?

Kann ich eine Gasflasche ausleihen? – Can I borrow a gas cylinder?

Complaints

Ich hätte gerne ein anderes Zimmer. - I would like a different room.

Die Heizung funktioniert nicht. - The heating does not work.

Die Klimaanlage funktioniert nicht. - The air conditioning does not work.

Das Zimmer ist sehr laut. - The room is very noisy.

Das Zimmer riecht komisch.- The room smells bad.

Ich habe um ein Nichtraucherzimmer gebeten. - I requested a non-smoking room.

Ich habe um ein Zimmer mit Ausblick gebeten. - I requested a room with a view.

Der Schlüssel funktioniert nicht. - My key does not work.

Das Fenster lässt sich nicht öffnen.- The window does not open.

Das Zimmer wurde nicht sauber gemacht. - The room has not been cleaned.

Es sind Mäuse/Ratten/Ungeziefer in meinem Zimmer.- There are mice / rats / bugs in the room.

Es gibt kein heißes Wasser. - There is no hot water.

Ich habe keinen Weckruf bekommen. - I did not receive my wake-up call.

Mir wurde zu viel berechnet. - The bill is overcharged.

Mein Nachbar ist zu laut. - My neighbour is too loud.

Important terms

check-in - Anmeldung

check-out - Abmeldung

reservation - Reservierung

vacanct room - freies Zimmer

to book - buchen

to check in - sich anmelden

to check out - sich abmelden

to pay the bill - Rechnung bezahlen

to stay at a hotel - in einem Hotel wohnen

hotel - Hotel

B&B - Zimmer mit Frühstück

Guesthouse - Gasthaus

Hostel - Hostel

Campsite - Campingplatz

single room - Einzelzimmer

double room - Doppelbettzimmer

twin room - Zweibettzimmer

triple room - Dreierzimmer

suite - Suite

air conditioning - Klimaanlage

bath - Badewanne

en-suite bathroom - Nasszelle

internet access - Internet Zugang

minibar - Minibar

safe - Safe

shower - Dusche

bar - Bar

car park - Parkplatz

corridor - Flur

fire escape - Feuerleiter

games room - Spieleraum

gym - Fitnessstudio

laundry service - Wäscheservice

lift - Aufzug

lobby - Lobby

reception - Rezeption

restaurant - Restaurant

room service - Zimmerservice

sauna - Sauna

swimming pool - Schwimmbecken

manager - Manager, Managerin

housekeeper - Reinigungskraft

receptionist - Rezeptionist, Rezeptionistin

room attendant - Zimmerservice
chambermaid - Zimmermädchen
doorman - Pförtner
porter - Portier
fire alarm - Feueralarm
laundry - Wäscherei
room key - Zimmerschlüssel
room number - Zimmernummer
wake-up call - Weckruf

Chapter 6 – Money

When you visit another country and have to deal with different currencies, it's very useful to know how to ask someone for help or for the price of something.

Akzeptieren Sie den amerikanischen/australischen/kanadischen Dollar? - Do you accept American/Australian/Canadian dollars?

Akzeptieren Sie das britische Pfund? - Do you accept British pounds?

Akzeptieren Sie den Euro? - Do you accept Euros?

Akzeptieren Sie Kreditkarten? - Do you accept credit cards?

Können Sie für mich Geld wechseln? - Can you change money for me?

Wo kann ich Geld wechseln? - Where can I get money changed?

Können Sie für mich Travelerchecks wechseln? - Can you change a traveler's check (USA)/ cheque (UK) for me?

Wo kann ich Travelerchecks wechseln? - Where can I get a traveler's check changed?

Wie ist der Wechselkurs? - What is the exchange rate?

Wo gibt es einen Geldautomaten? - Where is an automatic teller machine (ATM) (Amerik.) / cash dispenser (Brit.)?

Chapter 7 – Restaurants and Food

Tasting different foods and trying the local cuisine is certainly one of the best parts of visiting a foreign country. Before you sit down at a local restaurant before a big meal, you should of course take some time to find out how to talk to the waiter or waitress or how to order your dish. Many restaurants offer menus with translation, but if you also want to move beyond the tourist trails, you may have to come to terms with a German menu! Our list with some basic words and sentences will help you. The following phrases offer a great starting point:

Reservation and Ordering

Einen Tisch für eine Person/zwei Personen bitte. >> A table for one person/two people, please.

Könnte ich die Speisekarte haben? >> Can I look at the menu, please?

Kann ich die Küche sehen? >> Can I look in the kitchen?

Gibt es eine Hausspezialität? >> Is there a house specialty?

Gibt es eine lokale Spezialität? >> Is there a local specialty?

Ich bin Vegetarier. >> I'm a vegetarian.

Ich esse kein Schweinefleisch. >> I don't eat pork.

Ich esse kein Rindfleisch. >> I don't eat beef.

Ich esse nur koscheres Essen. >> I only eat kosher food.

Können Sie es fettarm kochen? >> Can you make it "lite," please?

Tagesmenü >> fixed-price meal
von der Karte >> a la carte
Frühstück >> breakfast
Mittagessen >> lunch
Teezeit >> tea
Abendessen >> dinner
Ich möchte _____. >> I would like _____.
Ich möchte Tischservice _____. >> I want a dish containing _____.
Huhn >> chicken
Rind >> beef
Fisch >> fish
Kochschinken >> ham
Wurst >> sausage
Käse >> cheese
Eier >> eggs
Salat >> salad
Gemüse >> vegetables
Früchte >> fruit
Brot >> bread
Toast >> toast
Glasnudeln >> noodles
Nudeln >> pasta
Reis >> rice
Bohnen >> beans
Kartoffel >> potato
Könnte ich ein Glas von_____haben? >> May I have a glass of _____?

Könnte ich eine Schale von _____ haben? >> May I have a cup of _____?

Könnte ich eine Flasche von _____ haben? >> May I have a bottle of _____?

Kaffee >> coffee

Tee >> tea

Saft >> juice

Mineralwasser >> water

Wasser >> water

Bier >> beer

Rotwein/Weisswein >> red/white wine

Könnte ich einige _____ haben? >> May I have some _____?

Salz >> salt

Schwarzpfeffer >> black pepper

Butter >> butter

Entschuldigung Kellner? >> Excuse me, waiter?

Ich bin fertig. >> I'm finished.

Es war hervorragend. >> It was delicious.

Bitte räumen Sie den Tisch ab. >> Please clear the plates.

Die Rechnung bitte. >> The check, please. / The bill, please/Can we pay, please

Ordering snacks

Haben Sie auch Snacks / Kleinigkeiten zu essen? - Do you have any snacks?

Haben Sie auch Sandwiches / belegte Brote? - Do you have any sandwiches?

Haben Sie auch etwas zu essen? - Do you serve food?

Wann schließt die Küche? - What time does the kitchen close?

Kann man bei Ihnen noch etwas essen? - Are you still serving food?

Eine Tüte (Germany)/Packerl (Austria) Chips, bitte – A packet of crisps, please.

Welche Geschmacksrichtung hätten Sie gern? - What flavour would you like?

Gesalzen - salted

Käse und Zwiebel - Cheese and onion

Salz und Essig - Salt and vinegar

Was für Sandwiches (belegte Brote) haben Sie? - What sort of sandwiches do you have?

Haben Sie auch warme Gerichte? - Do you have any hot food?

Die Tagesgerichte stehen auf der Tafel - Today's specials are on the board.

Wird man am Tisch bedient oder ist hier Selbstbedienung? - Is it table service or self-service?

Was kann ich dir bringen? - What can I get you?

Möchtest du gern etwas essen? - Would you like anything to eat?

Können wir bitte die Karte haben? - Could we see a menu, please?

If you order something in a cafe that accepts takeaway orders, you might be asked:

Zum hier Essen oder zum Mitnehmen? - Eat in or take-away?

Important terms

Fresh - frisch

Mouldy - schimmelig

Off - schlecht

Rotten - verrottet

Stale - alt

Juicy - saftig

Ripe - reif

Unripe - unreif
Tender - zart
Tough - zäh
over-done or over-cooked - verbrannt
under-done - nicht durch
bland - fad
delicious - hervorragend
horrible - schrecklich
poor - schlecht
salty - salzig
sickly sweet - zuckersüß
sweet - süß
sour - sauer
tasty - lecker
spicy or hot - scharf
mild - mild
to bake - backen
to boil - kochen
to fry - fritieren
to grill - grillen
to roast - braten
to steam - dünsten
breakfast - Frühstück
lunch - Mittagessen
tea - Tee
dinner - Abendessen
supper - Nachtmahl

to have breakfast - frühstücken

to have lunch - zu Mittag essen

to have dinner - zu Abend essen

ingredient - Zutat

recipe - Rezept

to cook - kochen

to lay the table or to set the table - den Tisch decken

to clear the table - den Tisch abräumen

to come to the table - sich an den Tisch setzen

to leave the table - den Tisch verlassen

to wipe the table - den Tisch abwischen

to prepare a meal - ein Gericht zubereiten

bar - die Bar

chef - der Koch, die Köchin

booking or reservation - die Reservierung

menu - die Speisekarte

waiter - der Kellner

waitress - die Kellnerin

wine list - die Weinkarte

starter - die Vorspeise

main course - das Hauptgericht

dessert - der Nachtisch

service - die Bedienung

service charge - der Bedienungsaufschlag

tip - das Trinkgeld

Chapter 8 – Bars

You can easily order your favorite drinks in a bar if you use these phrases below!

Ordering drinks

Servieren Sie Alkohol? >> Do you serve alcohol?

Gibt es einen Tischservice? >> Is there table service?

Ein Bier/zwei Biere bitte >> A beer/two beers, please.

Ein Glas Rotwein/Weisswein bitte. >> A glass of red/white wine, please.

Ein Glas bitte. >> A glass, please.

Ein halber Liter bitte. >> A pint, please.

Eine Flasche bitte. >> A bottle, please.

Whiskey >> whisky

Vodka >> vodka

Rum >> rum

Wasser >> water

Soda >> club soda

Tonic Wasser >> tonic water

Orangensaft >> orange juice

Coca Cola >> Coke

Haben Sie Snacks? >> Do you have any bar snacks?

Einen weiteren, bitte. >> One more, please.

Eine neue Runde bitte. >> Another round, please.

Wann schliessen Sie? >> When is closing time?

Was möchtest du trinken? - What would you like to drink?

Was nimmst du? - What are you having?

Was kann ich dir bringen? - What can I get you?

Ich hätte gern …, bitte - I'll have …, please

Ein großes Pils - a pint of lager

Ein großes Halbdunkles - a pint of bitter

Ein Glas Weißwein – A glass of white wine

Ein Glas Rotwein - A glass of red wine

Einen Orangensaft - An orange juice

Einen Kaffee - A coffee

Eine Cola - a Coke

Eine Cola Light - a Diet Coke

Groß oder klein? - Large or small?

Würde Sie es gerne mit Eis haben? - Would you like ice with that?

Kein Eis, bitte. - No ice, please.

Ein wenig, bitte - A little, please.

Eine Menge Eis, bitte - Lots of ice, please

Ein Bier, bitte - A beer, please.

Zwei Bier, bitte - Two beers, please.

Drei Tequilashots, bitte - Three shots of tequila, please.

Werden Sie schon bedient? - Are you already being served?

Danke, wir werden schon bedient - We're being served, thanks.

Der Nächste, bitte! - Who's next?

Welchen Wein hätten Sie gern? - Which wine would you like?

Ich nehme den Hauswein - House wine is fine.

Was für ein Bier möchten Sie haben? - Which beer would you like?

Möchten Sie es vom Fass oder aus der Flasche? - Would you like draught or bottled beer?

Ich nehme das Gleiche, danke - I'll have the same, please.

Für mich nichts, danke - Nothing for me, thanks.

Ich nehme diese hier - I'll get these.

Der Rest ist für Sie! - Keep the change!

Prost! - Cheers!

Wer ist dran mit der Runde? - Whose round is it?

Das ist meine Runde - It's my round.

Das ist deine Runde - It's your round.

Bitte noch ein Bier - Another beer, please.

Bitte noch zwei Bier – Another two beers, please.

Das Gleiche nochmal, bitte - Same again, please.

Schenken Sie noch Getränke aus? - Are you still serving drinks?

Letzte Bestellungen! - Last orders!

Asking for internet and WiFi

Haben Sie hier Internetzugang? - Do you have internet access here?

Haben Sie hier WiFi? – Do you have WiFi here?

Was ist das Passwort für das Internet? - What's the password for the internet?

The day after

Mir geht es gut - I feel fine.

Ich fühle mich furchtbar - I feel terrible.

Ich habe einen Kater - I've got a hangover.

Ich trinke nie wieder etwas! - I'm never going to drink again!

Smoking

Rauchst du?, rauchen Sie? - Do you smoke?

Nein, ich rauche nicht - No, I don't smoke.

Ich habe aufgehört - I've given up.

Stört es dich, wenn ich rauche? - Do you mind if I smoke?

Möchtest du eine Zigarette? - Would you like a cigarette?

Hast du ein Feuerzeug? - Have you got a lighter?

Do not forget to inform yourself beforehand about tipping practices. This is an essential part of a waiter's salary and should not be left out. However, the uses vary from country to country, so you should inform yourself before you travel.

Note: There is a very strong smoking culture in Austria, and as a result, bars and restaurants allow smokers to smoke on the premises. Sometimes there is a separate section for non-smokers, but not always!

Important terms

Cola/coke - Cola

fruit juice - Fruchtsaft

grapefruit juice - Grapefruitsaft

orange juice - Orangensaft

pineapple juice - Ananassaft

tomato juice - Tomatensaft

iced tea - Eistee

lemonade - Limonade

lime cordial - Limettengetränk

milkshake - Milchshake

orange squash - Orangensaftgetränk

pop - Limo
smoothie - Smoothie
squash-Fruchtsaftgetränk
water-Wasser
mineral water-Mineralwasser
still water-stilles Wasser
sparkling water-Sprudelwasser / Wasser mit Kohlensäure
tap water-Leitungswasser
cocoa-Kakao
coffee-Kaffee
black coffee-schwarzer Tee
decaffeinated coffee or decaf coffee-enkoffeinierter Kaffee
fruit tea-Früchtetee
green tea-grüner Tee
herbal tea-Kräutertee
hot chocolate-heiße Schokolade
tea-Tee
tea bag-Teebeutel
strong-stark
weak-schwach
ale-Dunkelbier
beer-Bier
bitter-Magenbitter
cider-Cider, Apfelwein
lager-Pils
shandy-Radler, Alsterwasser
stout-Dunkelbier, Starkbier

wine-Wein
red wine-Rotwein
white wine-Weißwein
rosé-Rosé
sparkling wine-Sekt
champagne-Champagner
martini-Martini
liqueur-Likör
brandy-Branntwein, Weinbrand
gin-Gin
rum-Rum
whisky, whiskey-Whisky
vodka-Wodka
alcohol-Alkohol
aperitif-Aperitif
bar-Theke
barman-Barkeeper
barmaid-Bardame
bartender-Barkeeper
beer glass-Bierglas
beer mat-Bierdeckel
binge drinking-Besäufnis
bottle-Flasche
can-Dose
cocktail-Cocktail
drunk-betrunken
hangover-Kater

pub-Kneipe

sober-nüchtern

spirits-Spirituosen

tipsy-beschwippst, angeheitert

wine glass-Weinglas

Chapter 9 – Shopping

You want to buy a few souvenirs quickly? Or maybe you need to buy groceries? To make shopping quick and problem-free, we have the most important phrases here:

Haben Sie das in meiner Grösse? > Do you have this in my size?

Wieviel kostet das? >> How much is this?

Das ist zu teuer. >> That's too expensive.

Wollen Sie _____ nehmen? >> Would you take _____?

teuer >> expensive

billig >> cheap

Ich kann es mir nicht leisten. >> I can't afford it.

Ich möchte es nicht. >> I don't want it.

Sie betrügen mich. >> You're cheating me.

Ich bin nicht interessiert >> I'm not interested.

OK, ich nehme es. >> OK, I'll take it.

Kann ich eine Tasche haben? >> Can I have a bag?

Versenden sie ? >> Do you ship ?

Haben Sie Übergrössen? >> Do you stock large sizes?

Ich brauche... >> I need...

...Zahnpasta. >> ...toothpaste.

...eine Zahnbürste. >> ...a toothbrush.

...Tampons. >> ...tampons.

...Seife. >> ...soap.

...Shampoo. >> ...shampoo.

...Schmerzmittel. >> ...pain reliever.

...Medizin gegen Erkältungen. >> ...cold medicine.

...Medizin für den Magen. >> ...stomach medicine.

...ein Rasierer. >> ...a razor.

...ein Regenschirm. >> ...an umbrella.

...Sonnencreme. >> ...sun lotion.

...eine Postkarte. >> ...a postcard.

...Briefmarken. >> ... stamps.

...Batterien. >> ...batteries.

...Schreibpapier. >> ...writing paper.

...ein Stift. >> ...a pen.

...englische Bücher. >> ...English-language books.

...eine englische Zeitschrift/Illustrierte. >> ...English-language magazines.

...eine englische Zeitung. <<===>> ...an English-language newspaper.

...ein englisch-X Wörterbuch. <<===>> ...an English-X dictionary.

Making a decision

Wie fühlen sie sich an? - How do they feel?

Sind sie bequem? - Do they feel comfortable?

Es steht Ihnen - It suits you.

Sie stehen Ihnen - They suit you.

Ist das die einzige Farbe, die Sie haben? - Is this the only colour you've got?

Was halten Sie von diesen hier? - What do you think of these?

Sie gefallen mir - I like them.

Sie gefallen mir nicht - I don't like them.

Die Farbe gefällt mir nicht - I don't like the colour.

Woraus sind sie gemacht? - What are these made of?

Kann man sie waschen? - Are these washable?

Nein, sie müssen in die Reinigung - No, they have to be dry-cleaned.

Ich nehme es - I'll take it.

Ich nehme sie - I'll take them.

Ich nehme das - I'll take this.

Ich nehme sie - I'll take these.

Finding products

Können Sie mir bitte sagen, wo ... ist? - Could you tell me where the ... is?

die Milch - milk

die Brottheke - bread counter

die Fleischabteilung - meat section

die Tiefkühlabteilung - frozen food section

Werden Sie schon bedient? - Are you being served?

Ich hätte gerne ... - I'd like ...

dieses Stück Käse - that piece of cheese

ein Stück Pizza - a slice of pizza

sechs Scheiben Schinken - six slices of ham

Ein paar Oliven - Some olives

Wieviel hätten Sie gerne? - How much would you like?

300 Gramm - 300 grams

Ein halbes Kilo, bitte - half a kilo

zwei Pfund (450 Gramm) - two pounds

Das macht €32.47 - that's €32.47

Kann ich bitte eine Tüte (Germany)/ ein Sackerl (Austria) haben? - Could I have a carrier bag, please?

Kann ich bitte noch eine Tüte/ ein Sackerl haben? - Could I have another carrier bag, please?

Brauchen Sie Hilfe beim Einpacken? - Do you need any help packing?

Haben Sie eine Kundenkarte? - Do you have a loyalty card?

At a hair salon

Ich hätte gerne einen Haarschnitt, bitte - I'd like a haircut, please.

Muss ich mir einen Termin ausmachen? - Do I need to book?

Kann ich gleich dableiben? - Are you able to see me now?

Möchten Sie gerne einen Termin ausmachen? - Would you like to make an appointment?

Möchten Sie die Haare gewaschen haben? - Would you like me to wash it?

Was möchten Sie? - What would you like?

Wie soll ich es schneiden? - How would you like me to cut it?

Das überlasse ich Ihnen - I'll leave it to you.

Ich hätte gern … - I'd like …

einen Nachschnitt - a trim

einen neuen Style - a new style

eine Dauerwelle - a perm

einen Pony - a fringe

Strähnen - some highlights

eine Färbung - it coloured

Bitte nur nachschneiden - Just a trim, please

Wie kurz hätten Sie es gern? - How short would you like it?

nicht zu kurz - not too short

ziemlich kurz - quite short

sehr kurz - very short

Stufe eins - grade one

Stufe zwei - grade two

Stufe drei - grade three

Stufe vier - grade four

komplett rasiert - completely shaven

Haben Sie einen Scheitel? - Do you have a parting?

Im Nacken gerade, bitte - Square at the back, please

Im Nacken zulaufend, bitte - Tapered at the back, please

Das ist in Ordnung, danke - That's fine, thanks

Welche Farbe möchten Sie? - What colour would you like?

Welche dieser Farben möchten Sie? - Which of these colours would you like?

Möchten Sie es geföhnt? - Would you like it blow-dried?

Können Sie mir bitte den Bart nachschneiden? - Could you trim my beard, please?

Können Sie mir bitte den Schnurrbart nachschneiden? - Could you trim my moustache, please?

Möchten Sie etwas ...? - Would you like anything on it?

Haarwachs - a little wax

Gel - some gel

Haarspray - some hairspray

Nein, danke - Nothing, thanks.

Wieviel bekommen Sie? - How much do I owe you?

Important terms

cheap-billig

customer-Kunde

discount-Rabatt
expensive-teuer
price-Preis
sale-Ausverkauf
shop-Laden
shopping bag-Einkaufstasche
shopping list-Einkaufsliste
special offer-Angebot
to buy-kaufen
to sell-verkaufen
to order-bestellen
to go shopping-einkaufen gehen

Im Laden
aisle-Gang
basket-Korb
counter-Ladentresen
fitting room-Ankleideraum
manager-Filialleiter
shelf-Regal
shop assistant-Ladenverkäufer
shop window-Ladenfenster
stockroom-Lagerraum
trolley-Einkaufswagen
cashier-Kassierer, Kassiererin
cash-Bargeld
change-Kleingeld
checkout-Kasse

complaint-Beschwerde

credit card-Kreditkarte

in stock-auf Lager

out of stock-nicht auf Lager

plastic bag or carrier bag-Plastiktüte

purse-Geldbeutel

queue-Schlange

receipt-Quittung

refund-Rückerstattung

till-Kasse

wallet-Brieftasche

Chapter 10 – Driving

If you plan on driving with your own car or renting one, then you should definitely know some rules and how to get to your destination without any issues. Here are some important phrases:

Könnte ich ein Auto mieten? >> Can I rent a car?

Kann ich eine Versicherung bekommen? >> Can I get insurance?

STOP >> stop

Einbahnstraße >> one way

Vorfahrt beachten >> yield

Parkverbot >> no parking

Höchstgeschwindigkeit >> speed limit

Tankstelle >> gas station /service station station

Benzin >> petrol /gas

Diesel >> diesel

Important terms

bypass-Umgehungsstraße

country lane-Landstraße

dual carriageway-zweispurige Schnellstraße

main road-Bundesstraße

motorway-Autobahn

one-way street-Einbahnstraße

ring road-Ortsumgehung

road-Straße

toll road-mautpflichtige Straße

Straßeneigenschaften

corner-Straßenecke

crossroads-Kreuzung

kerb-Bordstein

fork-Gabelung

hard shoulder-Seitenstreifen

junction-Kreuzung

lay-by-Parkstreifen

level crossing-Bahnübergang

pavement-Bürgersteig

pedestrian crossing-Fußgängerüberweg

road sign-Verkehrszeichen

roadside-Straßenrand

roadworks-Straßenarbeiten

roundabout-Kreisverkehr

services-Autobahnraststätte

signpost-Schild

speed limit-Geschwindigkeitsbegrenzung

T-junction-T-Kreuzung

toll-Maut

traffic light-Ampel

turning-abbiegen

accident-Unfall

breakdown-Panne

breathalyser-Alkoholtest-Röhrchen
jack-Wagenheber
jump leads-Starthilfekabel
flat tyre-Reifenpanne
fog-Nebel
icy road-vereiste Straße
puncture-Panne
speeding fine-Bußgeld wegen Geschwindigkeitsüberschreitung
spray-Spritzwasser
traffic jam-Verkehrsstau
to crash-zusammenstoßen
to have an accident-einen Unfall haben
to skid-rutschen
to stall-Motor abwürgen
to swerve-ausweichen
driving instructor-Fahrlehrer, Fahrlehrerin
driving lesson-Fahrstunde
driving licence-Führerschein
driving school-Fahrschule
driving test-Fahrprüfung
learner driver-Fahrschüler, Fahrschülerin
to fail your driving test- die Fahrprüfung durchfallen
to pass your driving test-die Fahrprüfung bestehen
car park-Parkplatz
disabled parking space-Behindertenparkplatz
multi-storey car park-Parkhaus
to park-parken

parking meter-Parkuhr

parking space-Stellplatz

parking ticket-Strafzettel

traffic warden-Polizeihelfer, Polizeihelferin

car wash-Autowaschstraße

diesel-Diesel

oil-Öl

petrol-Benzin

petrol pump-Benzinpumpe

petrol station-Tankstelle

unleaded-Bleifrei-Benzin

bike-Fahrrad

camper van-Wohnmobil

bus-Bus

car-Auto

caravan-Wohnwagen

coach-Reisebus

lorry-Lastwagen

minibus-Minibus

moped-Moped

motorbike-Motorrad (informell)

scooter-Motorroller

taxi-Taxi

tractor-Traktor

truck-Lastwagen (amerikanisches Englisch)

van-Van

car hire-Autoverleih

car keys-Autoschlüssel
cyclist-Fahrradfahrer
driver-Fahrer, Fahrerin
garage-Werkstatt
mechanic-Mechaniker, Mechanikerin
insurance-Versicherung
passenger-Beifahrer
pedestrian-Fußgänger
reverse gear-Rückwärtsgang
road map-Straßenkarte
second-hand-gebraucht
speed-Geschwindigkeit
traffic-Verkehr
tyre pressure-Reifendruck
vehicle-Fahrzeug
to accelerate-beschleunigen
to brake-bremsen
to change gear-schalten
to drive-fahren
to overtake-überholen
to reverse-rückwärts fahren
to slow down-abbremsen
to speed up-beschleunigen
to steer-lenken
accelerator-Gaspedal
brake pedal-Bremse
clutch pedal-Kupplung

fuel gauge-Tankanzeige
gear stick-Schaltknüppel
handbrake-Handbremse
speedometer-Tachometer
steering wheel-Lenkrad
temperature gauge-Temperaturanzeige
warning light-Warnlicht
Mechanische Teile
battery-Batterie
brakes-Bremsen
clutch-Kupplung
engine-Motor
fan belt-Keilriemen
exhaust-Auspuff
exhaust pipe-Auspuffrohr
gear box-Getriebe
ignition-Zündung
radiator-Kühler
spark plug-Zündkerze
windscreen wiper-Scheibenwischer
air conditioning-Klimaanlage
automatic-Automatik
central locking-Zentralverriegelung
manual-Handschaltung
tax disc-Steuerplakette
sat nav-Satellitennavigation
brake light-Bremslicht

hazard lights-Warnblinker
headlamp-Scheinwerfer
indicators-Blinker
rear view mirror-Rückspiegel
sidelights-Standlicht
wing mirror-Seitenspiegel
Andere Teile
aerial-Antenne
back seat-Rücksitz
bonnet-Motorhaube
boot-Kofferraum
bumper-Stoßstange
child seat-Kindersitz
cigarette lighter-Zigarettenanzünder
dashboard-Armaturenbrett
front seat-Vordersitz
fuel tank-Kraftstofftank
glove compartment-Handschuhfach
glovebox-Handschuhfach
heater-Heizung
number plate-Kennzeichen
passenger seat-Beifahrersitz
petrol tank-Benzintank
roof-Dach
roof rack-Dachgepäckträger
seatbelt-Anschnallgurt
spare wheel-Ersatzreifen

tow bar-Abschleppstange

tyre-Reifen

wheel-Rad

window-Fenster

windscreen-Windschutzscheibe

Chapter 11 – Authorities

If you have to deal with authorities, it's good to know some of the phrases to explain yourself and get out of a difficult situation.

Ich habe nichts falsch gemacht. >> I haven't done anything wrong.

Es war ein Missverständniss. >> It was a misunderstanding.

Wohin bringen Sie mich? >> Where are you taking me?

Nehmen Sie mich fest? >> Am I under arrest?

Ich bin ein amerikansicher/australischer/britischer/kanadischer Staatsangehöriger. >> I am an American/Australian/British/Canadian citizen.

Ich bin ein deutscher/österreichischer/schweizer Staatsangehöriger. >> I am a German/Austrian/Swiss citizen.

Ich will mit der amerikanischen/australischen/britischen/kanadischen Botschaft/Konsulat sprechen. >> I need to talk to the American/Australian/British/Canadian embassy/consulate.

Ich möchte mit einem Anwalt sprechen. >> I want to talk to a lawyer.

Kann ich nicht einfach eine Buße bezahlen? >> Can't I just pay a fine now?

Chapter 12 – Emergencies

In case of an emergency, make sure to use these phrases:

Hilfe! - Help!

Feuer! - Fire!

Bitte gehen Sie! – Please go away!

Ich rufe die Polizei. - I'll call the police.

Es ist dringend! - It's urgent!

Ich bin vom Weg abgekommen. - I'm lost.

Ich habe ... - I've lost…

meinen Reisepaß verloren. - my passport.

meinen Autoschlüssel verloren. - my car keys.

Ich bin ausgeraubt worden. - I've been robbed.

Ich hatte einen Unfall. - I've had an accident.

Mein Auto hatte eine Panne. - My car has broken down.

Mein Auto ist gestohlen worden. - My car has been stolen.

Der Kühler wurde zu heiß. – The radiator has overheated.

Der Reifen ist geplatzt. - The tire has a puncture.

Die Batterie ist leer. - The battery is flat.

Die Kupplung ist defekt. - The clutch is broken.

Die Bremsen funktionieren nicht. - The brakes are not working.

Ich weiß nicht, woran es liegt. - I don't know what the problem is.

Ich brauche ... - I need…

Benzin. - Some petrol..

einen Mechaniker. - A mechanic.

die Polizei. - The police

Health

Ich brauche ... - I need…

einen Arzt. - a doctor.

ein Telefon. - A telephone.

einen Krankenwagen. - An ambulance.

einen Dolmetscher. - An interpreter.

Wo ist das Krankenhaus? - Where is the hospital?

Ich bin allergisch gegen Penizillin. - I'm allergic to penicillin.

Ich bin ... - I'm…

Diabetiker. - diabetic.

Asthmatiker. - asthmatic.

Ich brauche ... - I need…

einen Optiker. - An optician.

einen Zahnarzt. - A dentist.

Hier habe ich Schmerzen. - It hurts here.

Ich glaube, er/sie/es ist gebrochen. - I think it's broken.

At the pharmacy

Ich hätte gern ... - I'd like some …

Zahnpasta - toothpaste

Paracetamol - paracetamol

Ich habe ein Rezept - I've got a prescription here from the doctor.

Haben Sie etwas gegen …? - have you got anything for …?

Herpesbläschen - cold sores

Halsschmerzen - a sore throat

rissige Lippen - chapped lips

Husten - a cough

Reiseübelkeit - travel sickness

Fußpilz - athlete's foot

Können Sie etwas gegen eine Erkältung empfehlen? - Can you recommend anything for a cold?

Ich habe ... - I'm suffering from ...

Heuschnupfen - hay fever

Verdauungsstörungen - indigestion

Durchfall - diarrhoea

Ich habe Ausschlag - I've got a rash.

Sie können diese Salbe ausprobieren - You could try this cream.

Wenn es nach einer Woche nicht weg ist, sollten Sie zum Arzt gehen - If it doesn't clear up after a week, you should see your doctor.

Haben Sie etwas, dass mir dabei hilft, mit dem Rauchen aufzuhören? - Have you got anything to help me stop smoking?

Haben Sie schon einmal Nikotinpflaster ausprobiert? - Have you tried nicotine patches?

Kann ich das hier rezeptfrei bekommen? - Can I buy this without a prescription?

Das gibt es nur auf Rezept - It's only available on prescription.

Hat es irgendwelche Nebenwirkungen? - Does it have any side-effects?

Es kann Sie schläfrig machen - It can make you feel drowsy.

Sie sollten keinen Alkohol trinken - You should avoid alcohol.

Kann ich bitte mit dem Apotheker sprechen? - I'd like to speak to the pharmacist, please.

Visiting a doctor

Ich möchte einen Doktor/Arzt sehen - I'd like to see a doctor.

Haben Sie einen Termin? - Do you have an appointment?

Ist es dringend? - Is it urgent?

Ich hätte gern einen Termin bei Dr. ... - I'd like to make an appointment to see Dr ...

Gibt es hier einen Arzt der ... spricht? - Do you have any doctors who speak ...?

Englisch - English

Sind Sie privat versichert? - Do you have private medical insurance?

Haben Sie eine Europäische Krankenversicherungkarte? - Have you got a European Health Insurance card?

Bitte nehmen Sie Platz - Please take a seat.

Der Arzt kann Sie jetzt sehen - The doctor's ready to see you now.

Was kann ich für Sie tun? - How can I help you?

Worin besteht Ihr Problem? - What's the problem?

Was für Symptome haben Sie? - What are your symptoms?

Ich habe ... - I've got a ...

Fieber - temperature

Halsschmerzen - sore throat

Kopfschmerzen - headache

Ausschlag - rash

Ich fühle mich seit einer Weile nicht wohl - I've been feeling sick.

Ich habe seit einer Weile Kopfschmerzen - I've been having headaches.

Meine Nase ist verstopft - I'm very congested.

Ich habe Gelenkschmerzen - My joints are aching.

Ich habe Durchfall - I've got diarrhea.

Ich habe Verstopfung - I'm constipated.

Ich habe eine Beule - I've got a lump/bump.

Ich habe einen geschwollenen ... - I've got a swollen ...

Knöchel - ankle

Ich habe starke Schmerzen - I'm in a lot of pain.

Ich habe ... - I've got a pain in my ...

Rückenschmerzen – back pain

Schmerzen in meiner Brust – chest pain

Ich glaube, ich habe mir einen Muskel in meinem Bein gezerrt - I think I've pulled a muscle in my leg.

Ich brauche ... - I need ...

neues Asthmaspray - another inhaler

etwas mehr Insulin - some more insulin

Ich habe Schwierigkeiten beim Atmen - I'm having difficulty breathing.

Ich fühle mich sehr schwach - I've got very little energy.

Ich bin seit einer Weile sehr müde - I've been feeling very tired.

Ich fühle mich seit einer Weile deprimiert - I've been feeling depressed.

Ich habe seit einer Weile Schlafstörungen - I've been having difficulty sleeping.

Wie lange fühlen Sie sich schon so? - How long have you been feeling like this?

Wie fühlen Sie sich im Allgemeinen? - How have you been feeling generally?

Besteht die Möglichkeit einer Schwangerschaft? - Is there any possibility you might be pregnant?

Ich bin möglicherweise schwanger - I think I might be pregnant.

Haben Sie irgendwelche Allergien? - Do you have any allergies?

Ich bin gegen Antibiotika allergisch - I'm allergic to antibiotics.

Nehmen Sie irgendwelche Medikamente? - Are you on any sort of medication?

Ich brauche eine Krankschreibung - I need a sick note.

Darf ich mir das mal ansehen? - Can I have a look?

Wo tut es weh? - Where does it hurt?

Es tut hier weh - It hurts here.

Tut es weh, wenn ich hier Druck ausübe? - Does it hurt when I press here?

Ich werde ... messen - I'm going to take your ...

Ihren Blutdruck - blood pressure

Ihre Temperatur - temperature

Ihren Puls - pulse

Können Sie bitte Ihren Ärmel hochkrempeln? - Could you roll up your sleeve?

Ihr Blutdruck ist ... - Your blood pressure's ...

ziemlich niedrig - quite low

normal - normal

ziemlich hoch - rather high

sehr hoch - very high

Ihre Temperatur ist ... - Your temperature's ...

normal - normal

leicht erhöht - a little high

sehr hoch - very high

Machen Sie bitte den Mund auf - Open your mouth, please.

Bitte husten Sie - Cough, please.

Sie werden ein paar Stiche brauchen - You're going to need a few stiches.

Ich werde Ihnen eine Spritze geben - I'm going to give you an injection.

Wir müssen eine ... nehmen - We need to take a ...

Urinprobe - urine sample

Blutprobe - blood sample

Sie müssen eine Blutuntersuchung machen lassen - You need to have a blood test.

Ich werde Ihnen Antibiotika verschreiben - I'm going to prescribe you some antibiotics.

Nehmen Sie davon dreimal täglich zwei - Take two of these pills three times a day.

Gehen Sie mit diesem Rezept zur Apotheke - Take this prescription to the chemist.

Rauchen Sie? - Do you smoke?

Sie sollten mit dem Rauchen aufhören - You should stop smoking.

Wieviel Alkohol trinken Sie pro Woche - How much alcohol do you drink a week?

Sie sollten das Trinken einschränken - You should cut down on your drinking.

Sie sollten versuchen, Ihr Gewicht zu reduzieren - You need to try and lose some weight.

Ich möchte Sie gern zum Röntgen schicken - I want to send you for an x-ray.

Ich möchte, dass Sie einen Spezialisten aufsuchen - I want you to see a specialist.

Important terms

aftershave-Aftershave

comb-Kamm

conditioner-Haarspülung

dental floss-Zahnseide

deodorant-Deodorant
hairbrush-Haarbürste
mouthwash-Mundspülung
nail file-Nagelfeile
nail scissors-Nagelschere
panty liners-Slipeinlage
perfume-Parfüm
razor-Rasierer
razorblade-Rasierklinge
sanitary towels-Damenbinden
shaving brush-Rasierpinsel
shaving cream-Rasiercreme
shaving foam-Rasierschaum
shaving gel-Rasiergel
shampoo-Shampoo
shower gel-Duschgel
soap-Seife
tampons-Tampons
toothbrush-Zahnbürste
toothpaste-Zahncreme
tweezers-Pinzette
cotton wool-Watte
eyeliner-Eyeliner
eyeshadow-Lidschatten
face powder-Gesichtspuder
foundation-Grundierung, Foundation
hair colouring or hair dye-Haarfarbe, Haartönung

hair gel-Haargel

hair spray-Haarspray

hair wax-Haarwachs

hand cream-Handcreme

lip gloss-Lipgloss

lipstick-Lippenstift

make-up-Makeup

mascara-Wimperntusche

moisturising cream-Feuchtigkeitscreme

nail varnish-Nagellack

nail varnish remover-Nagelackentferner

antiseptic-Antiseptikum

aspirin-Aspirin

athlete's foot powder-Fußpilzpuder

bandages-Bandagen

cough mixture-Hustensaft

diarrhoea tablets-Durchfalltabletten

emergency contraception - die Pille danach

eye drops-Augentropfen

first aid kit-Erste-Hilfe-Ausrüstung

hay fever tablets-Tabletten gegen Heuschnupfen

indigestion tablets-Tabletten gegen Magenverstimmungen

laxatives-Abführmittel

lip balm oder lip salve-Lippenbalsam

medicine-Medizin

nicotine patches-Nikotinpflaster

painkillers-Schmerzmittel

paracetamol-Paracetamol

plasters-Pflaster

pregnancy testing kit-Schwangerschaftstest

prescription-Rezept, Verschreibung

sleeping tablets-Schlaftabletten

thermometer-Thermometer

throat lozenges-Hustenpastille

tissues-Taschentücher

travel sickness tablets-Tabletten gegen Reisekrankheit

vitamin pills-Vitamintabletten

baby foods-Babynahrung

baby wipes-Babytücher

condoms-Kondome

contact lens solution-Kontaktlinsenlösung

disposable nappies-Wegwerfwindeln

hot water bottle-Wärmflasche

safety pins-Sicherheitsnadel

sun cream-Sonnencreme

sun block-Sonnenblocker, Sun-Blocker

beard-Bart

cheek-Wange

chin-Kinn

head-Kopf

hair-Haar

ear-Ohr

eye-Auge

eyebrow-Augenbraue

eardrum-Trommelfell
earlobe-Ohrläppchen
eyelash-Wimper
eyelid-Augenlid
forehead-Stirn
freckles-Sommersprossen
jaw-Kiefer
lip-Lippe
mouth-Mund
nose-Nase
nostril-Nasenloch
moustache-Schnurrbart
tongue-Zunge
tooth (Plural: teeth)-Zahn
wrinkles-Falten
Adam's apple-Adamsapfel
arm-Arm
armpit-Achsel
back-Rücken
breast-Brust, Busen
chest-Brust, Brustkorb
elbow-Ellbogen
hand-Hand
finger-Finger
fingernail-Fingernagel
forearm-Unterarm
knuckle-Knöchel

navel or belly button-Bauchnabel
neck-Hals
nipple-Nippel
palm-Handfläche
shoulder-Schulter
throat-Rachen
thumb-Daumen
waist-Taille
wrist-Handgelenk
ankle-Fußgelenk
anus-Anus
belly-Bauch
big toe-große Zeh
bottom-Po
buttocks-Gesäß
calf-Wade
foot (Plural: feet)-Fuß
genitals-Genitalien
groin-Leiste
heel-Ferse
hip-Hüfte
knee-Knie
leg-Bein
penis-Penis
pubic hair-Schamhaar
shin-Schiene
sole-Sohle

testicles-Hoden

thigh-Oberschenkel

toe-Zeh

toenail-Zehnagel

vagina-Vagina

cornea-Augenhornhaut

eye socket-Augenhöhle

eyeball-Augapfel

iris-Iris

retina-Retina

pupil-Pupille

Achilles tendon-Achillessehne

artery-Arterie

appendix-Blinddarm

bladder-Blase

blood vessel-Blutgefäß

brain-Gehirn

cartilage-Knorpel

colon-Darm

gall bladder oder gallbladder-Galle

heart-Herz

intestines-Eingeweide

large intestine-Dickdarm

small intestine-Dünndarm

kidneys-Nieren

ligament-Band

liver-Leber

lungs-Lunge

oesophagus-Speiseröhre

pancreas-Bauchspeicheldrüse

organ-Organ

prostate gland oder prostate-Prostata

rectum-Enddarm

spleen-Milz

stomach-Bauch, Magen

tendon-Sehne

tonsils-Mandeln

vein-Vene

windpipe-Luftröhre

womb oder uterus-Gebärmutter

collarbone oder clavicle-Schlüsselbein

thigh bone oder femur-Oberschenkelknochen

humerus-Oberarmknochen

kneecap-Kniescheibe

pelvis-Becken

rib-Rippe

rib cage-Brustkorb

skeleton-Skelett

skull-Schädel

spine oder backbone-Wirbelsäule

vertebra (Plural: vertebrae)-Wirbel

Körperflüssigkeiten

bile-Galle

blood-Blut

mucus-Schleim

phlegm-Phlegma

saliva oder spit-Speichel

semen-Samen

sweat oder perspiration-Schweiß

tears-Tränen

urine-Urin

vomit-Erbrochenes

Andere verwandte Wörter

bone-Knoche

fat-Fett

flesh-Fleisch

gland-Drüse

joint-Gelenk

limb-Extremität

muscle-Muskel

nerve-Nerv

skin-Haut

digestive system-Verdauungstrakt

nervous system-Nervensystem

to breathe-atmen

to cry-weinen

to hiccup-aufstoßen

to have the hiccups-Schluckauf haben

to sneeze-nießen

to sweat oder to perspire-schwitzen

to urinate-urinieren

to vomit-erbrechen/speiben

to yawn-gähnen

smell-Geruchssinn

touch-Tastsinn

sight-Sehen

hearing-Gehör

taste-Geschmackssinn

to smell-riechen

to touch-anfassen

to see-sehen

to hear-hören

to taste-schmecken

Chapter 13 - Services and repairs

If you have personal items that require repair or cleaning, these phrases will be helpful.

Können Sie mir sagen, wo ich ... zur Reparatur bringen kann? - Do you know where I can get my ... repaired?

Telefon/Handy – phone/mobile phone

meine Uhr - my watch

mein Fotoapparat - camera

meine Schuhe - shoes

Der Bildschirm ist kaputt - The screen's broken.

Mit ... stimmt was nicht - There's something wrong with ...

meiner Uhr - my watch

diesem Radio - this radio

Reparieren Sie ...? - Do you do ... repairs?

Fernseher - television

Computer - computer

Laptops - laptop

Was wird es ungefähr kosten? - How much will it cost?

Wann wird es fertig sein? - When will it be ready?

Wie lange wird es dauern? - How long will it take?

Ich kann es jetzt gleich erledigen - I can do it straight away

... ist es fertig - it'll be ready ...

bis morgen - by tomorrow

bis nächste Woche - next week

Innerhalb der nächsten zwei Wochen werde ich es nicht schaffen - I won't be able to do it for at least two weeks.

Können Sie es reparieren? - Are you able to repair it?

Wir können es nicht selbst machen - We can't do it here.

Wir müssen es zurück zum Hersteller schicken - We're going to have to send it back to the manufacturers.

Eine Reparatur lohnt sich nicht - It's not worth repairing.

Meine Uhr ist stehengeblieben - My watch has stopped.

Darf ich mal sehen? - Can I have a look at it?

Ich glaube, sie braucht eine neue Batterie - I think it needs a new battery.

Ich wollte ... abholen - I've come to collect my ...

meine Uhr - watch

meinen Computer - computer

Photography

Könnten Sie die Fotos auf dieser Speicherkarte für mich drucken? - Could you print the photos on this memory card for me?

Könnten Sie die Fotos auf diesem Memorystick für mich drucken? - Could you print the photos on this memory stick for me?

Möchten Sie die Bilder in Matt oder Hochglanz? - Would you like matte or gloss prints?

Welche Größe sollen die Bilder haben? - What size prints would you like?

Post office

Wie viel kostet eine Briefmarke für einen Eilbrief? - How much is a first class stamp?

Wie viel kostet eine Briefmarke für eine normale Sendung? - How much is a second class stamp?

Ich hätte gern ..., bitte - I'd like ..., please

Einen Briefumschlag - an envelope

ein Paket Briefumschläge - a packet of envelopes

einen gepolsterten Briefumschlag - a jiffy bag

Könnte ich bitte ... haben? - Could I have ..., please?

eine Briefmarke für einen Eilbrief? - a first class stamp

eine Briefmarke für eine normale Sendung? - a second class stamp

ein Briefmarkenheft für Eilbriefe - a book of first class stamps

einige Briefmarken für Eilbriefe - some first class stamps

Wie viele hätten Sie gerne? - How many would you like?

Wie viele sind in einem Heft? - How many are there in a book?

Ich möchte das hier nach ... schicken - I'd like to send this to ...

Ich möchte dieses Paket nach ... schicken - I'd like to send this parcel to ...

Wieviel kostet dieser Brief nach/in die ...? - How much will it cost to send this letter to ...?

Würden Sie es bitte auf die Waage legen? - Can you put it on the scales, please?

Ich würde diesen Brief gerne per ... verschicken - I'd like to send this letter by ...

Einschreiben - Recorded Delivery

Eilbrief mit Versicherung - Special Delivery

Wo ist der Briefkasten? - Where's the postbox?

Wann muss ich das hier spätestens nach / in die ... abschicken, damit es rechtzeitig zu Weihnachten ankommt? - What's the last date I can post this to ... to arrive in time for Christmas?

Ich würde gerne ein Paket abholen - I've come to collect a parcel.

Ich würde gerne diese Rechnung bezahlen - I'd like to pay this bill.

Ich möchte gern Geld nach ... transferieren - I'd like to send some money to ...

Verkaufen Sie ...? - Do you sell ...?

Postkarten - postcards

Geburtstagskarten - birthday cards

Weihnachtskarten - Christmas cards

Ich möchte gern meinen Fernseher anmelden - I'd like to get a TV licence.

Ich möchte gern meine Fernsehlizenz verlängern - I need to renew my TV licence.

Würden Sie bitte dieses Formular ausfüllen? - Can you fill in this form, please?

Haben Sie ...? - Do you have a ...?

einen Fotoautomaten - photo booth

einen Fotokopierer - photocopier

Bank

Ich möchte gern einhundert Euro abheben, bitte - I'd like to withdraw €100, please.

Ich möchte gern Geld abheben - I want to make a withdrawal.

Wie hätten Sie es gern? - How would you like the money?

in Zehnern, bitte - in tens, please

Könnten Sie mir ein paar kleinere Scheine geben? - Could you give me some smaller notes?

Ich wüder das gerne einzahlen, bitte - I'd like to pay this in, please.

Ich möchte gern diesen Scheck einlösen, bitte - I'd like to pay this check in, please.

Wie lange dauert es bis der Scheck eingelöst ist? - How many days will it take for the check to clear?

Haben Sie …? - Have you got any …?

einen Ausweis dabei - identification

Ich habe … - I've got my …

meinen Pass dabei - passport

meinen Führerschein dabei - driving licence

meinen Personalausweis dabei - ID card

Ihr Konto ist überzogen - Your account's overdrawn.

Ich würde gerne Geld auf dieses Konto überweisen - I'd like to transfer some money to this account.

Könnten Sie bitte tausend Euro von meinem Girokonto auf mein Sparkonto überweisen? - Could you transfer €1000 from my current account to my deposit account?

Ich möchte ein Bankkonto eröffnen - I'd like to open an account.

Ich möchte ein Privatkonto eröffnen - I'd like to open a personal account.

Ich möchte ein Geschäftskonto eröffnen - I'd like to open a business account.

Können Sie mir bitte meinen Kontostand sagen? - Could you tell me my balance, please?

Könnte ich bitte einen Kontoauszug haben? - Could I have a statement, please?

Ich möchte gern etwas Geld wechseln - I'd like to change some money.

Ich möchte gern Fremdwährung bestellen - I'd like to order some foreign currency.

wie lautet der Wechselkurs für Euro? - What's the exchange rate for euros?

Ich hätte gern ... - I'd like some ...

Euro - euros

US-Dollar - US dollars

Kann ich bitte ein neues Scheckbuch haben? - Could I order a new checkbook, please?

Ich möchte einen Scheck zurückziehen - I'd like to cancel a check.

Ich möchte diesen Dauerauftrag beenden - I'd like to cancel this standing order.

Wo ist der nächste Geldautomat/Bankomat? - Where's the nearest cash machine?

Wie hoch ist der Zinssatz für dieses Konto? - What's the interest rate on this account?

Wie hoch ist der aktuelle Zinssatz für Privatkredite? - What's the current interest rate for personal loans?

Ich habe meine Bankkarte verloren - I've lost my bank card.

Ich möchte eine ... melden - I want to report a ...

verlorene Kreditkarte - lost credit card

gestohlene Kreditkarte - stolen credit card

Wir haben ein gemeinsames Konto - We've got a joint account.

Ich möchte gern eine Adressänderung melden - I'd like to tell you about a change of address.

Ich habe das Passwort für mein Online-Konto vergessen - I've forgotten my Internet banking password.

Ich habe die PIN für meine Karte vergessen - I've forgotten the PIN number for my card.

Ich werde Ihnen ein neues senden - I'll have a new one sent out to you.

Ich hätte gern einen Termin mit ... - Could I make an appointment to see ...?

dem Geschäftsführer - the manager

einem Finanzberater - a financial advisor

Ich hätte gern eine Beratung zum Thema Hypothek - I'd like to speak to someone about a mortgage.

ATM

Führen Sie ihre Karte ein - Insert your card.

Geben Sie ihre PIN ein - Enter your PIN.

Falsche PIN - Incorrect PIN

Eingabe - Enter

Korrektur - Correct

Abbruch - Cancel

Bargeld abheben - Withdraw cash

Anderer Betrag - Other amount

Bitte warten - Please wait

Ihr Geld wird gezählt - Your cash is being counted.

Kontostand nicht ausreichend - Insufficient funds

Kontostand - Balance

Auf dem Bildschirm - On screen

Ausgedruckt - Printed

Weiterer Dienst? - Another service?

Wollen Sie eine Rechnung haben? - Would you like a receipt?

Karte entnehmen - Remove card.

Verlassen - Quit

Important terms

laptop-Laptop

desktop computer-Computer

tablet computer-Tablet

PC-PC

screen-Bildschirm

keyboard-Tastatur

mouse-Maus

monitor-Bildschirm

printer-Drucker

wireless router-WLAN Router

cable-Kabel

hard drive-Festplatte

speakers-Lautsprecher

power cable-Stromkabel

email-E-Mail

to email-e-mailen

to send an email-eine E-Mail senden

email address-E-Mailadresse

username-Benutzername

password-Passwort

to reply-antworten

to forward-weiterleiten

new message-neue Nachricht

attachment-Anhang

to plug in-einstecken

to unplug-ausstöpseln

to switch on or to turn on-anmachen

to switch off or to turn off-ausmachen

to start up-hochfahren

to shut down-herunterfahren

to restart-erneut einschalten

the Internet-das Internet

website-Webseite

broadband internet or broadband-Breitband-Internet

ISP-Internetdienstanbieter

firewall-Firewall

web hosting-Webhosting

wireless internet or WiFi-drahtloses Netz oder WLAN

to download-herunterladen

to browse the Internet-im Internet suchen

Andere nützliche Wörter

file-Datei

folder-Verzeichnis

document-Dokument

hardware-Hardware

software-Software

network-Netzwerk

to scroll up-nach oben scrollen

to scroll down-nach unten scrollen

to log on-einloggen

to log off-ausloggen

space bar-Leertaste

virus-Virus

antivirus software-Antiviren-Software

processor speed-Prozessorgeschwindigkeit

memory-Speicher

word processor-Textverarbeitungsprogramm

database-Datenbank

spreadsheet-Kalkulationstabelle

to print-drucken

to type-tippen

lower case letter-Kleinbuchstaben

upper case letter oder capital letter-Großbuchstaben

Chapter 14 – Spare Time

When you have spare time, you'll probably visit the theater, museum or club. Whatever the case is, these phrases may help you:

Teathre

Läuft … etwas in Theater? - Is there anything on at the theatre …?

heute Abend - tonight

diese Woche - this week

diesen Monat - this month

Wie lange läuft das Stück noch? - When's the play on until?

Wer spielt darin mit? - Who's in it?

Was für ein Stück ist es? - What type of production is it?

Es ist … - It's …

eine Komödie - a comedy

eine Tragödie - a tragedy

ein Musical - a musical

eine Oper - an opera

ein Ballet - a ballet

Hast du das Stück schon mal gesehen? - Have you seen it before?

Um wieviel Uhr beginnt die Vorstellung? - What time does the performance start?

Wann ist es zuende? - What time does it finish?

Wo ist die Garderobe? - Where's the cloakroom?

Möchten Sie gern ein Programmheft? - Would you like a program?

Kann ich bitte ein Programmheft haben? - Could I have a program, please?

Sollen wir für die Pause etwas zu trinken bestellen? - Shall we order some drinks for the interval?

Wir sollten zu unseren Plätzen zurückgehen - We'd better go back to our seats.

Hat es dir gefallen? - Did you enjoy it?

The club

Hast du Lust, heute abend in die Disco zu gehen? - Do you want to go to a club tonight?

Kennst du eine gute Disco hier in der Nähe? - Do you know any good clubs near here?

Bis wann haben Sie geöffnet? - What time are you open until?

Wann schließen Sie? - What time do you close?

Was kostet der Eintritt? - How much is it to get in?

Gibt es eine Kleiderordnung? - Is there a dress code?

An welchen Abenden haben Sie geöffnet? - What nights are you open?

Was für eine Art Musik spielen Sie? - What sort of music is it?

Was gibt es heute Abend? - What's on tonight?

Gibt es heute Abend Livemusik bei Ihnen? - Do you have any live music tonight?

Sorry, Sie können nicht rein - Sorry, you can't come in.

Sie können nicht mit Turnschuhen rein - You can't come in with trainers on.

Heute Nacht ist eine Privatparty - There's a private party tonight.

Der Klub ist voll - The club's full.

Ich bin auf der Gästeliste - I'm on the guest list.

Ich bin ein Mitglied - I'm a member.

Wo ist die Garderobe? - Where's the cloakroom?

Wie gefällt dir der DJ? - What do you think of the DJ?

Die Musik ist super - The music's great!

Es ist viel los heute Abend - It's very lively tonight.

Es ist ein bisschen leer - It's a bit empty.

Ziemlich tote Hose hier (Slang) - It's dead in here.

Wo ist die Bar? - Where's the bar?

An der Bar ist eine lange Schlange - There's a long queue at the bar.

Es ist zu laut - It's too loud.

Es ist zu heiss hier drinnen - It's too hot in here.

Möchtest du nach Hause gehen? - Are you ready to go home?

Ich gehe nach Hause - I'm going home.

Flirting – Small Talk

Kann ich mich setzen? - May I join you?

Darf ich Dir ein Getränk ausgeben? - May I buy you something to drink?

Bist Du oft hier? - Do you come here often?

Und, was machst du beruflich? - So, what do you do for a living?

Willst Du tanzen? - Do you want to dance?

Möchtest du kurz rausgehen? - Would you like to get some fresh air?

Willst Du auf eine andere Party gehen? - Do you want to go to a different party?

Lass uns losgehen! - Let's get out of here!

Zu mir oder zu dir? - My place or yours?

Möchtest Du bei mir einen Film schauen? - Would you like to watch a movie at my place?

Hast Du heute Abend etwas vor? - Do you have any plans for tonight?

Würdest Du mit mir mal Mittagessen/Abendessen gehen? - Would you like to have lunch/dinner with me sometime?

Würdest Du mit mir einen Kaffee trinken gehen? - Would you like to go get a coffee?

Kann ich Dich nach Hause begleiten/fahren? - May I walk/drive you home?

Würdest Du Dich gern noch einmal treffen? - Would you like to meet again?

Danke für den schönen Abend. Gute Nacht! - Thank you for a lovely evening!

Möchtest Du auf einen Kaffee hereinkommen? - Would you like to come inside for a coffee?

Du siehst hinreißend aus! - You're gorgeous!

Du bist lustig! - You're funny!

Du hast wunderschöne Augen! - You have beautiful eyes!

Du bist eine gute Tänzerin/ein guter Tänzer! - You're a great dancer!

Du siehst wunderschön in dem Kleid/T-Shirt/Hemd aus! - You look beautiful in that dress/shirt!

Ich habe den ganzen Tag an Dich gedacht! - I have been thinking about you all day!

Es war schön, mit Dir zu reden! - It's been really nice talking to you!

Ich habe kein Interesse. - I'm not interested.

Lass mich in Ruhe. - Leave me alone.

Verschwinde/Hau ab! - Get lost!

Fass mich nicht an! - Don't touch me!

Nimm deine Finger weg! - Get your hands off me!

Museum and Gallery

Was kostet der Eintritt? - How much is it to get in?

Kostet es Eintritt? - Is there an admission charge?

Nur für die Ausstellung - Only for the exhibition.

Wann schließen Sie? - What time do you close?

Das Museum ist montags geschlossen - The museum's closed on Mondays.

Darf ich fotografieren? - Can I take photographs?

Möchten Sie einen Audio-Guide? - Would you like an audio-guide?

Gibt es heute geführte Touren? - Are there any guided tours today?

Wann beginnt die nächste geführte Tour? - What time does the next guided tour start?

Wo ist die Garderobe? - Where's the cloakroom?

Wir müssen unsere Taschen an der Garderobe abgeben - We have to leave our bags in the cloakroom.

Haben Sie einen Übersichtsplan des Museums? - Do you have a plan of the museum?

Wer hat dieses Bild gemalt? - Who's this painting by?

Dieses Museum hat eine sehr gute Sammlung von … - This museum's got a very good collection of …

Ölgemälden - oil paintings

Aquarellen - watercolours

Porträts - portraits

Landschaftsbildern - landscapes

Skulpturen - sculptures

antiken Kunstgegenständen - ancient artifacts

Keramik - pottery

magst du …? - do you like …?

moderne Kunst - modern art

klassische Gemälde - classical paintings

impressionistische Gemälde - impressionist paintings

Important terms

avenue-Allee

bus shelter-Wartehäuschen

bus stop-Bushaltestelle

high street-Haupteinkaufsstraße

lamppost-Laternenpfahl

parking meter-Parkuhr

pavement-Bürgersteig

pedestrian crossing-Fußgängerüberweg

pedestrian subway-Fußgängerunterführung

side street-Seitenstraße

signpost-Hinweisschild

square-Platz

street-Straße

taxi rank-Taxistand

telephone box oder telephone booth-Telefonhäuschen

antique shop-Antiquitätenladen

bakery-Bäckerei

barbers-Frisörsalon für Männer

beauty salon-Schönheitssalon

betting shop or bookmakers-Wettbüro

bookshop-Buchhandlung

butchers-Metzgerei

car showroom-Autohändler

charity shop-Gebrauchtwarenladen, dessen Umsatz für wohltätige Zwecke bestimmt ist

chemists oder pharmacy-Apotheke

clothes shop-Bekleidungsgeschäft

delicatessen-Feinkostgeschäft

department store-Kaufhaus

DIY store-Baumarkt

dress shop-Bekleidungsgeschäft

dry cleaners-Trockenreinigung

electrical shop-Elektronikgeschäft

estate agents-Immobilienbüro

fishmongers-Fischhändler

florists-Blumenladen

garden centre-Gartenzentrum

general store-Gemischtwarenladen

gift shop-Geschenkartikelladen

greengrocers-Gemüsehändler

hairdressers-Frisörsalon

hardware shop-Eisenwarenladen

kiosk-Kiosk

launderette-Waschsalon

newsagents-Zeitschriftenladen

off licence-Wein- und Spirituosenhandlung

second-hand bookshop-Antiquariat

second-hand clothes shop-Second-Hand-Laden

shoe repair shop-Schuhreperatur

shoe shop-Schuhgeschäft

sports shop-Sportgeschäft

stationers-Schreibwarengeschäft

supermarket-Supermarkt

tailors-Schneider

tattoo parlor or tattoo studio-Tattooladen

toy shop-Spielzeugladen

apartment block-Wohnblock

art gallery-Kunstgalerie

bank-Bank

bar-Bar

block of flats-Mietshaus

building society-Wohnungsbaugesellschaft

café-Café

cathedral-Kathedrale

church-Kirche

cinema-Kino

concert hall-Konzerthalle

dentists-Zahnarzt

doctors--Arzt

fire station-Feuerwehr

fish and chip shop-Pommesbude

chestnuts and potatoes stand – Maronistand

garage-Garage; Autowerkstatt

gym-Fitnessstudio

health centre-Gesundheitszentrum

hospital-Krankenhaus

hotel-Hotel

internet cafe-Internet Café

leisure centre oder sports centre-Freizeitzentrum

library-Bücherei

mosque-Moschee

museum-Museum

office block-Bürogebäude

petrol station-Tankstelle

police station-Polizeiwache

post office-Postamt

pub-Kneipe

restaurant-Restaurant

school-Schule

shopping centre-Einkaufszentrum

skyscraper-Wolkenkratzer

swimming baths-Schwimmbad

synagogue-Synagoge

theatre-Theater

tower block-Hochhaus

town hall-Rathaus

university-Universität

vets-Tierarzt

wine bar-Weinbar

bowling alley-Bowlinghalle

bus station-Busbahnhof

car park-Parkplatz

cemetery-Friedhof

children's playground-Spielplatz

marketplace-Marktplatz

multi-storey car park-Parkhaus

park-Park

skate park-Skatepark

stadium-Stadion

town square-zentraler Platz

train station-Bahnhof

zoo-Zoo

Chapter 15 – Useful words and terms

Here are some useful words and their translation so you can quickly express your thoughts:

Landscape and geographical terms

countryside-Land

hill-Hügel

mountain-Berg

valley-Tal

wood-Wald

forest-Wald (große Fläche)

copse-Hain

field-Feld

meadow-Wiese

plain-Ebene

moor-Heide

bog-Moor

swamp-Sumpf

hedge-Hecke

path-Pfad

fence-Zaun

wall-Mauer

ditch-Graben
gate-Tor
farm-Bauernhof
bridge-Brücke
desert-Wüste
glacier-Gletscher
jungle-Dschungel
rainforest-Regenwald
volcano-Vulkan
stream-Bach
river-Fluss
canal-Kanal
pond-Teich
lake-See
reservoir-Reservoir
waterfall-Wasserfall
well-Brunnen
dam-Damm
power station-Elektrizitätswerk
wind farm-Windfarm
mine-Miene
quarry-Steinbruch
agriculture-Landwirtschaft
barn-Scheune
farmhouse-Bauernhaus
crop-Getreide
harvest-Ernte

hay-Heu
wheat-Weizen
irrigation-Bewässerung
livestock-Vieh
to plough-pflügen
to harvest-ernten
ocean-Ozean
sea-Meer
coast oder shore-Küste
beach-Strand
cliff-Kliff
island-Insel
peninsula-Halbinsel
rock-Fels
tide-Gezeiten
wave-Welle
pier-Pier
lighthouse-Leuchtturm
harbour-Hafen
oil rig-Ölbohrplattform
Other useful words-Andere nützliche Wörter
country-Land
city-Stadt (Großstadt)
town-Stadt
village-Dorf
eruption-Ausbruch
earthquake-Erdbeben

tsunami-Tsunami
avalanche-Lawine
landslide-Erdrutsch
lava-Lava
capital city oder capital-Hauptstadt
border-Grenze
national park-Nationalpark
North Pole-Nordpol
South Pole-Südpol
Equator-Äquator
longitude-Längengrad
latitude--Breitengrand
sea level-Meeresspiegel
erosion-Erosion
pollution-Verschmutzung
atmosphere-Atmosphäre
environment-Umwelt
population-Bevölkerung
famine-Hungersnot
fossil fuel-fossiler Brennstoff
energy-Energie
unemployment-Arbeitslosigkeit
landscape-Landschaft
literacy-Fähigkeit zu lesen
malnutrition-Unterernährung
migration-Völkerwanderung
radiation-Strahlung

nuclear energy-Atomenergie

crater-Krater

sand dune-Sanddüne

trade-Handel

urban-urban

rural-ländlich

economy-Wirtschaft

poverty-Armut

slum-Armutsviertel

life expectancy-Lebenserwartung

The weather

sun-Sonne

sunshine-Sonnenschein

rain-Regen

snow-Schnee

hail-Hagel

drizzle-Nieselregen

sleet-Schneeregen

shower-Regenschauer

mist-leichter Nebel

fog-dichter Nebel

cloud-Wolke

rainbow-Regenbogen

wind-Wind

breeze-Brise

strong winds-starker Wind

thunder-Donner

lightning-Blitz

storm-Sturm

thunderstorm-Gewitter

gale-starker Wind, Sturm

tornado-Tornado

hurricane-Hurrikan

flood-Flut, Überschwemmung

frost-Frost

ice-Eis

drought-Dürre

heat wave-Hitzewelle

windy-windig

cloudy-bewölkt

foggy-neblig (dicht)

misty-neblig (leicht)

icy-eisig

frosty-frostig

stormy-stürmisch

dry-trocken

wet-nass

hot-heiß

cold-kalt

chilly-kühl

sunny-sonnig

rainy-regnerisch, verregnet

fine-schön

dull-bedeckt

overcast-bewölkt

humid-feucht

raindrop-Regentropfen

snowflake-Schneeflocke

hailstone-Hagelkorn

to melt-schmelzen

to freeze-frieren

to thaw-tauen

to snow-schneien

to rain-regnen

to hail-hageln

weather forecast-Wettervorhersage

rainfall-Niederschlag

temperature-Temperatur

humidity-Luftfeuchtigkeit

thermometer-Thermometer

high pressure-Hochdruck

low pressure-Tiefdruck

barometer-Barometer

degree-Grad

Celsius--Celsius

Fahrenheit-Fahrenheit

Home appliance

battery-Batterie

candle-Kerze

cotton-Baumwolle

envelopes-Briefumschläge

firelighters-Feueranzünder
fuse-Sicherung
glue-Klebstoff
light bulb-Glühbirne
lighter-Feuerzeug
matches-Streichhölzer
needle-Nadel
safety pin-Sicherheitsnadel
scissors-Schere
sellotape-Klebestreifen, Tesafilm
stamps-Briefmarken
pen-Kugelschreiber
pencil-Bleistift
tissues-Taschentücher
toilet paper oder toilet roll-Toilettenpapier
toothpaste-Zahnpasta
tube of toothpaste-Zahnpastatube
writing paper-Schreibpapier
bin bag oder bin liner-Müllbeutel
bleach-Bleiche
detergent-Spülmittel
disinfectant-Desinfektionsmittel
dustbin bag-Müllsack
duster-Staublappen
fabric softener-Weichspüler
floorcloth-Putzlappen
furniture polish-Möbelpolitur

hoover bag-Staubsaugerbeutel
shoe polish-Schuhwichse
soap-Seife
washing powder-Waschpulver

Animals

dog-Hund
cat-Katze
rabbit- Kaninchen
hamster-Hamster
goldfish-Goldfisch
cow-Kuh
sheep (Plural: sheep)-Schaf
pig-Schwein
horse-Pferd
chicken-Hühnchen
fox-Fuchs
deer (Plural: deer)-Hirsch
mouse (Plural: mice)-Maus
rat-Ratte
frog-Frosch
snake-Schlange
lion-Löwe
tiger-Tiger
monkey-Affe
elephant-Elefant
giraffe-Giraffe
bear-Bär

pigeon-Taube

crow-Krähe

dove-Taube

owl-Eule

eagle-Adler

ant-Ameise

fly-Fliege

spider-Spinne

bee-Biene

wasp-Wespe

butterfly-Schmetterling

cod (Plural: cod)-Kabeljau

trout (Plural: trout)-Forelle

salmon (Plural: salmon)-Lachs

tuna (Plural: tuna)-Thunfisch

shark-Hai

crab-Krabbe

tail-Schwanz

fur-Fell

claw-Klaue

paw-Tatze

hoof-Huf

mane-Mähne

trunk-Rüssel

snout-Schnauze

Flowers

bracken-Farnkraut

brambles-Brombeerstrauch
bush-Busch
cactus (Plural: cacti)-Kaktus
corn-Mais
fern-Farn
flower-Blume
grass-Gras
heather-Heide
herb-Kraut
ivy-Efeu
moss-Moos
mushroom-Pilz (gewöhnlich essbar)
nettle-Nessel
shrub-Strauch
thistle-Distel
toadstool-Giftpilz
tree-Baum
weed-Unkraut
wheat-Weizen
wild flower-Wildblume
bluebell-Hasenglöckchen
buttercup-Butterblume
carnation-Nelke
chrysanthemum-Chrysantheme
crocus-Krokus
daffodil-Osterglocke
dahlia-Dahlie

daisy-Gänseblümchen
dandelion-Löwenzahn
forget-me-not-Vergissmeinnicht
foxglove-Fingerhut
geranium-Geranie
lily-Lilie
orchid-Orchidee
pansy-Stiefmütterchen
poppy-Mohn
primrose-Schlüsselblume
rose-Rose
snowdrop-Schneeglöckchen
sunflower-Sonnenblume
tulip-Tulpe
waterlily-Weiße Seerose
bouquet of flowers oder flower bouquet-Blumenstrauß
bunch of flowers-Blumenstrauß
berry-Beere
blossom-Blüte
bud-Knospe
flower-Blüte
leaf-Blatt
petal-Blütenblatt
pollen-Pollen
root-Wurzel
stalk-Stiel
stem-Stamm

thorn-Dorn
alder-Erle
ash-Esche
beech-Buche
birch-Birke
cedar-Zeder
elm-Ulme
fir-Tanne
hazel-Hasel
hawthorn-Weissdorn
holly-Stechpalme
lime-Linde
maple-Ahorn
oak-Eiche
plane-Platane
pine-Kiefer
poplar-Pappel
sycamore-Sycamore
weeping willow-Trauerweide
willow-Weide
yew-Eibe
apple tree-Apfelbaum
cherry tree-Kirschbaum
chestnut tree-Kastanienbaum
coconut tree-Kokonusspalme
fig tree-Feigenbaum
horse chestnut tree-Rosskastanie

olive tree-Olivenbaum

pear tree-Birnenbaum

plum tree-Pflaumenbaum

bark-Rinde

branch-Ast

pine cone-Kiefernzapfen

sap-Pflanzensaft

tree stump oder stump-Baumstumpf

trunk-Baumstamm

twig-Zweig

fruit tree-Obstbaum

palm tree-Palme

evergreen-immergrün

coniferous-zapfentragend

deciduous-laubabwerfend

Useful adjectives

big-groß

small oder little-klein

fast-schnell

slow-langsam

good-gut

bad-schlecht

expensive-teuer

cheap-billig

thick-dick

thin-dünn

narrow-eng

wide-breit
broad-breit
loud-laut
quiet-leise
intelligent-intelligent
stupid-dumm
wet-nass
dry-trocken
heavy-schwer
light-leicht
hard-hart
soft-weich
shallow-flach, seicht
deep-tief
easy-leicht
difficult-schwierig
weak-schwach
strong-stark
rich-reich
poor-arm
young-jung
old-alt
long-lang
short-kurz
high-hoch
low-tief
generous-großzügig

mean-geizig
true-richtig
false-falsch
beautiful-schön
ugly-hässlich
new-neu
old-alt
happy-fröhlich, glücklich
sad-traurig
safe-sicher
dangerous-gefährlich
early-früh
late-spät
light-hell
dark-dunkel
open-offen, geöffnet
closed oder shut-geschlossen, zu
tight- fest
loose-locker
full-voll
empty-leer
many-viele
few-wenige
alive-lebendig
dead-tot
hot-heiß
cold-kalt

interesting-interessant
boring-langweilig
lucky-glücklich
unlucky-unglücklich
important-wichtig
unimportant-unwichtig
right-richtig
wrong-falsch
far-weit
near-nahe
clean-sauber
dirty-schmutzig
nice-nett
nasty-gemein
pleasant-angenehm
unpleasant-unangenehm
excellent-ausgezeichnet
terrible-schrecklich
fair-fair
unfair-unfair
normal-normal
abnormal-anormal

Chapter 16 – Tips for learning a new language

Are you in the middle of planning your trip? Did you think of everything? First aid kit, papers & documents? Very good, but what about your foreign language skills? Have you ever thought how you'll express yourself? Unfortunately, many travelers neglect this topic and think that with English you can get anywhere. And some also assume that you can communicate well with your hands and feet. The question that you should ask yourself is:

What do I expect from my journey and which goal do I have?

To give you a little motivation, here are 5 advantages of being able to express yourself in the foreign language.

-You get to know the locals much more authentically.

-You understand the culture and attitude of people much better.

-You can negotiate more effectively.

-You do not waste valuable time, because you understand faster.

-You feel safer.

Just to keep it short: You do not have to learn the foreign language to perfection. But you should be able to communicate well. Here are some tips on how to learn certain basics quickly and effectively.

Are you ready? Okay, then we can start. Depending on how much time you have until the trip, you should use the time well. Which language level you achieve depends entirely on you. Here are some essential recommendations on how to learn a language.

1. Speak from the first day.

Unfortunately, many people follow a wrong approach when learning a language. A language is a means of communication and should therefore be lived rather than learned. There is no such thing as an "I am ready now." Therefore, just jump into the cold water and speak already at home from the first day on. That sounds horrible and silly? It does not matter, with time it will get better. It is best to set the goal not to miss a day when you have not used the foreign language in any form. Just try to implement everything you learn directly. So speak, write and think in your foreign language.

2. Immerse yourself in the foreign language at home.

This tip actually goes hand in hand with the first recommendation. To learn the foreign language quickly and efficiently, you have to integrate it firmly into your everyday life. It is not enough if you learn a few words from time to time and engage in grammar and pronunciation. This has to be done much more intensively. You have to dive properly into the foreign language. Just bring foreign countries to your home. By so-called "Immersion" you surround yourself almost constantly and everywhere with the learning language.

3.Change the language setting on devices.

For example, you could change the menu language of your smartphone or laptop from your native language to your learning language. Since you use your smartphone or your laptop every day, you know where to find something and learn some vocabulary along the way. Of course you can also do the same with your social networks like Facebook and Twitter. But watch out that you are always able to change back the menu language!

4.Use foreign language media.

You could, for example, get a foreign language newspaper. If that is not available or too expensive, then there are enough newspapers or news portals where you can read news online. Probably you are already familiar with the news through your native language, then the context is easier if you read the same messages again in the foreign language. Further aids are foreign-language films or series. It's probably best to start with a movie or series that you've already seen in your native language. The slang and common phrases can make it really hard for you. If you realize that you are not understanding it well, try the subtitle in the foreign language. If that does not work, then take the subtitle of your native language and try again. Even music should not be neglected in your foreign-language world. This has the advantage of teaching you a lot about the pronunciation and emphasis. Incidentally, you are getting a lot closer to the culture of the country.

5. Set notes in your apartment

If it does not bother you and others, spread little sticky notes with words in the apartment. Whether this is your toothbrush, the couch or the remote control, just place notes on as many objects and pieces of furniture as possible with the respective name of the object in the foreign language. As a result, you have the vocabulary all day long and memorize it automatically.

6. Learn the most important phrases

Another helpful tip is to think about what words and phrases you'll need before you travel. For example, you could write down how to reserve a hotel room or book a bus ride. Even how to order in the restaurant, ask someone for directions and how to communicate with the doctor or the police. Of course, this book is more than enough and you have all the phrases at one place.

7. Set clear goals

Last but not least, an important piece of advice: Set clear goals. Without goals, you will never get where you want to go. Since you have already booked your flight, you also have a deadline, to which you have reached a goal you have set. To accomplish this, you can now place mini orders. But stay realistic with your goals, especially in relation to your mini goals. If they are too big and not realistically achievable, you may lose your courage and give up. A good tip is also that you record your goals in writing because writing is like having a contract with yourself. It makes your goals more binding and makes you feel more obligated to stick to your schedule. The writing down also has the advantage that you have to formulate your goals more precisely and not forget them so quickly. Do not just try to formulate these goals, but really approach them and implement them.

Here are some examples of how you could define your goals:

Learn 300 words

Memorize 5 phrases

Write an email in the foreign language

Memorize important questions

Conduct a talk online via webcam

How can you achieve your goals?

Set Priorities: Be sure to rank your goals by importance!

Stay realistic: What is your current life situation?

Start today: Do not think about tomorrow or yesterday, but start today to reach your goals! The longer you wait, the less likely you are to achieve your goals.

Tell others about it: If others know about your goals, then you will do everything possible to reach them. Otherwise, you would have to admit defeat. This tip could of course make you stress, but will help you to work purposefully!

Change your habits: You may need to change something in your daily routine to achieve your goals. Do not hesitate and reject bad habits that get in your way!

Reward yourself: Every time you reach a partial goal, do something good! You know best what that can be!

Obviously, you do not have to punish yourself, but some people are more likely to do it than to be rewarded for success.

Let the imagination play: Imagine how it is when you reach your goals. What would you be capable of? What would you feel? This will motivate you immensely to work on your goals!

8. Humor

Do not feel sad, if it does not work right away. You may be embarrassing yourself in front of a native speaker because you mispronounce a word and make a completely different sense. Nobody will blame you. For most people it means a lot that you try to learn their language. And when they laugh then they do not mean that. But the most important thing is: have fun getting to know a new language! After all, you do not have any pressure, as you do at school.

Mastering the foreign language of your destination country has only advantages. You will learn to understand how people of a particular region think, what fears and worries they have and how they tackle life. You'll become more tolerant and see the world differently and, after your journey, you'll definitely question many ways of thinking of your own culture. Of course, you will also learn a lot of new things abroad, even in foreign languages. But please take the time already and get familiar with the new language before you leave. We promise you, it's worth it!

Chapter 17 – Bonus – Writing an e-mail

Maybe you need to make an appointment or write an e-mail to the manager of the hotel you are staying in, or maybe you are writing to your friend in Germany. In this chapter, we show you how to properly write an e-mail in German.

A formal letter

Start your letter with the word "Sehr geehrte/r Herr/Frau" followed by the last name of the person you are writing to. For example:

Sehr geehrter Herr Schmidt,

Sehr geehrte Frau Schmidt,

Here are some things you could write:

Danke für … - Thanks for your …

Ihren Brief - letter

Ihre Postkarte - postcard

Ihr Geschenk - present

Ihre Einladung - invitation

Entschuldigen Sie bitte, dass ich mir mit der Antwort so lange Zeit gelassen habe. - Sorry it's taken me so long to write.

Ich hoffe es geht Ihnen gut. - I hope you're well.

Es war schön, Sie letzte Woche zu sehen. - Good to see you again last week.

Ich freue mich Sie bald wieder zu sehen. - Look forward to seeing you soon!

Here are some ways to finish a formal letter:

Alles Gute, - Best regards,

Viele Grüße, - Kind regards,

End the letter with your last name.

Write an E-Mail

E-mails, whether business or private, are usually written in a more informal style than letters.

You should always give your email a subject that describes its purpose in a few words.

There are different guidelines for how business emails should be started. However, it is common to use the first name in both business and private emails, as long as you know the recipient.

It is not necessary to use "Lieber" (Dear), although some prefer this. Generally, business emails should be kept short. If you are sending, remember to mention them in the text of your e-mail. To end a private email, you can use the same expressions as for informal letters. There are different guidelines for how you should end your business emails. In general, the following expressions are appropriate:

Gruß, - Regards,

Freundliche Grüße, - Kind regards,

Mit besten Grüßen, - Best regards,

Mit freundlichen Grüßen, - With kind regards,

In business emails, you should continue to add your full name, organization, and contact information at the end.

Write a formal e-mail

If you know the addressee's name, start your letter with Sehr geehrter Herr (for a man), Sehr geehrte Frau (for a woman), followed by the surname.

Here are some things you could write in a formal e-mail:

Ich beziehe mich in diesem Schreiben auf Ihren Brief vom 4. September, bezüglich Ihrer unbezahlten Rechnung. - I am writing in reply to your letter of 4 September regarding your outstanding invoice.

Bezug nehmend auf unser Gespräch möchte ich gerne unseren Termin am Dienstag, 7. Januar um 09:30 Uhr bestätigen. - Further to our conversation, I'm pleased to confirm our appointment for 9.30am on Tuesday, 7 January.

Ich wäre Ihnen sehr dankbar, wenn Sie sich der Angelegenheit baldmöglichst annehmen würden. - I would be grateful if you could attend to this matter as soon as possible.

Wenn Sie weitere Informationen wünschen, zögern Sie bitte nicht, sich mit mir in Verbindung zu setzen. - If you would like any further information, please don't hesitate to contact me.

If you want an answer, you can use one of the following expressions at the end of your letter:

Ich freue mich darauf, von Ihnen zu hören. - I look forward to hearing from you.

If you started the letter with Sehr geehrter Herr/Frau, you should finish it as follows:

Mit freundlichen Grüßen, - Yours sincerely,

Mit freundlichen Grüßen, - Yours faithfully,

Add your signature at the end, followed by your full name.

Conclusion

Learning a language perfectly in two weeks on vacation is impossible. So it's not worth trying? Maybe you also believe that your language skills are not good enough to speak to the locals. You're wrong!

No matter how well you speak the language, even a short vacation can be a real boost for your language skills. But you have to do it right. Just going on holiday and watching what "happens" will usually lead to disappointment.

So how do you manage to get the most out of your vacation, no matter how low or high your language level is? Before traveling abroad, you should make the right preparations. So you make sure that it really works. The more you speak German on your holiday, the more you'll be comfortable with the language.

Sometimes talking to locals can be extremely difficult, especially if your language level is not quite as high. It can happen that people have no patience with you to have a conversation. Nevertheless, there are many ways to talk to the locals in the local language. It does not always have to be highly complex conversations. There are also opportunities to have short and easy talks, because even those help you with your language skills.

As a beginner or if you are not so sure about the language, you should have a short and simple conversation. This works best with people who have no other choice but to talk to you – like the waiter in restaurants, a barkeeper, receptionists in hotels, couriers and similar.

This is why you'll have everything you need in this book. You have to insist on speaking in the local language. If not, explain briefly that you would like to practice the language a bit. Almost everyone will understand.

And lastly, don't be afraid. It's okay to make mistakes. Everyone makes them. Make sure you don't forget this phrasebook on your trip and you'll be fine!

Preview of German
An Essential Guide to German Language Learning

Introduction

Whatever plans you may have for your future, with knowledge of the German language, you can create infinite possibilities. Learning German means acquiring skills to improve your professional and personal quality of life.

A global career: With German-language skills, you can improve your career prospects with German companies in your own country and in other countries. Good German skills make you a productive employee for an employer with global business relationships.

Tourism and hotel accommodation: Tourists from German-speaking countries travel far and wide, spending more on holiday than tourists from other countries. They are gladly introduced by German-speaking staff and German-speaking tour guides.

Science and research: German is the second most important language for science. With its contribution to research and development, Germany is third in the world in grant research fellowships to foreign scientists.

Communication: The developments in the media and information and communication technology require multilingual communication. A number of important websites are in German. Germany is ranked 6th in the world out of 87 countries, (just behind India, the UK, the USA, China and Russia) in the annual production of new books. Your knowledge of the German language, therefore, allows you to access more information.

Cultural understanding: Learning German means gaining an insight into the life, the wishes, and the dreams of people in German-speaking countries, with their multicultural society.

Travel: With your knowledge of German, you can expand your travel experiences not only in the German-speaking countries, but also in other European countries, especially Eastern Europe.

Enjoyment of literature, music, art and philosophy: German is the language of Goethe, Kafka, Mozart, Bach and Beethoven. Speaking German allows you to deepen the enjoyment of reading and / or listening of their works in their original language.

Study and work opportunities in Germany: Germany awards a large number of scholarships to study there. There are special visas for young foreigners, and there are special provisions for work permits for certain professions.

Exchange programs: There are exchange programs between students from Germany and many countries around the world.

In business life: Communication in German with your German-speaking business partners leads to better business relations and thus to better opportunities for effective communication - and thus to success.

All these reasons and more are why learning German is a great idea. Start your journey with this amazing book!

Chapter 1 – Pronunciation

Learning the German alphabet

The basis of any language is its alphabet. It would be kind of embarrassing if you could speak a language, but you couldn't really spell your own name. In this chapter, you will have the opportunity to learn what you absolutely need to know about the German alphabet, and you will get answers to questions such as:

What is a "Umlaut?"

When to use "ß" and when "ss?"

How do you pronounce "sch" and "ch?"

The German alphabet has 26 letters, just like the English alphabet. In addition, there are the following "umlauts" (gray): Ü, Ö, Ä and the ß.

A, Ä, B, C, D, E, F, G, H, I, J, K, L, M, N, O, Ö, P, Q, R, S, ß, T, U, Ü, V, W, X, Y, Z

Alphabet with pronunciation A/a [a:]

Ä/ä [ɛ:]

B/b [be:]

C/c [tse:]

D/d [de:]

E/e [e:]

F/f [ɛf]

G/g [Ge]

H/h [HA]

I/i [i]

J/j [jɔt]

K/k [ka:]

L/l [ɛl]

M/m [ɛm]

N/n [ɛn]

O/o [o:]

Ö/ö [O]

P/p [pe:]

Q/q [ku:]

R/r [ɛr]

S/s [ɛs]

ß [ɛs'tsɛt]

T/t [te:]

U/u [u:]

Ü/ü [y:]

V/v [faʊ]

W/w [unit:]

X / x [ICS]
Y / y [ˈiupsilɔn]
Z / z [t͡sɛt]

Vowels

In the German alphabet there are 8 vowels.

A, E, I, O and U, and 3 Umlauts, Ä, Ü, Ö.

These are formed by two successive vowels:

Ü,ü   U+E (Bücher)

Ä, ä   A+E (Länder)

Ö,ö   O+E (Brötchen)

Diphthongs

Diphthongs are two consecutive vowels. "Ei" and "ai" sound the same, like "eu" and "äu." To figure out when to use which diphthong, it is helpful to form the word stem. "Mäuse (Mice)," for example, is formed from "Maus (Mouse)"; therefore the plural is formed with "au" instead of "eu." The diphthong "ei" is used much more frequently than the diphthong "ai" If you do not know which of the two to use, use the "ei," because the probability of getting it right is significantly higher. The "ie" is pronounced as a long "i." Again, it is difficult to know when it is a simple "I," and when it is an "ie."

Diphthong pronunciation examples:

EI/AI - as the English "I" - **I**ron/M**y**

IE – as the "e" in English – F**ee**l

EU/ÄU - similar to the "oi" in "to boil"

AU - similar to the "ou" in "to bounce"

Ss or ß?

The ß (Esszett) is formed from a double "s"; it is a so-called "voiceless s." The Eßzett is used only after a long vowel, if one must consider whether one must use a double "s." For example, a sharp "s" is not used for "Lesen (read)" or "Rasen (lawn)." Unfortunately, there is no simple rule with which you can learn when to use the ß and when the ss. But the words with ß are limited. As long as you memorize them, you will be successful.

Here are a few common examples:

Spaß - fun

Straße - street

Gruß - greeting

Floß - raft

Heißen - be called

Groß - big

The "sch" and "ch"

The "ch" does not really exist in English. There are two different ways that Germans pronounce the "ch." The "sch" is almost always pronounced the same. The only exception is the letter sequence "ssch," which is pronounced as a double "s" and "ch" separated.

Ch - after "a, o, u, au" – in the back of the mouth – Bach

Ch - after "e, i, eu, ei, ä, ö, ü, äu, ai", or consonant like the "h" in "huge" – Fichte

Sch - always the same, (exception "ssch" (bisschen)) - like the "sh" in English

Letter case

German is not hard to learn. You just need to remember that all nouns and names are capitalized. Verbs and adjectives, as well as pronouns and conjugations, are lower case. As you have already noticed in this chapter, every word at the beginning of the sentence is capitalized after a point.

Summary

After completing this part, you should be able to spell your name. If a "ch" or "sch" occurs in your name, you now know how to pronounce it in German!

Exercises

1. Find and highlight the words containing "ch," which is pronounced like the "h" in "huge".

Heute Morgen bin ich um elf aufgewacht. Ich hatte Pech, denn ich habe den Wecker nicht gehört. Heute werde ich einfach zuHause bleiben. Vielleicht kann ich auch einen Film sehen. Es ist in Ordnung, wenn man sich ein bisschen von allem erholen will. Morgen ist wieder ein neuer Tag. Mein Vater holt mich ab und wir werden in einen Wald voller Fichten gehen. Vielleicht werden wir auch meine Schwester mitnehmen.

2. Insert the correct word from the parenthesis into the space.

a) _____ (Eulen/Äulen) sind sehr interessante Tiere.

b) Hier gibt es viele _____ (Heuser/Häuser).

c) Im _____ (Mei/Mai) hat _____ (meine/maine) Mutter Geburtstag.

d) Am Freitag _____ (flige/fliege) ich nach Italien.

e) Es ist wirklich _____ (heiß/haiß) draußen.

3. Insert the correct word.

a) Der _____ (Hund/hund) muss zum Tierarzt.

b) ___ (ich/Ich) bin sehr hungrig.

Hast du heute _____ (deine/Deine) Mutter gesehen?

c) Mein bester _____ (Freund/ freund) hat heute Geburtstag.

d) Hast du ____ (Lust/lust) mit mir spazieren zu gehen?

e) _____ (Heute/heute) ist ein sehr schöner Tag.

Chapter 2 – The basics

Nouns - main words

Mann, Hund, Katze, Maus: Nouns. In German, Nomen (nouns; also called "Hauptwort") is a word category. It refers to living beings, things, or facts. Nouns in German are always capitalized. In this chapter, you'll learn everything you need to know about nouns.

Why do I recognize the gender of a noun? That will determine which of the three common German articles (der, die, das) you have to use, which is a bit confusing for everyone who learns German as a foreign language.

How to form the plural of a noun? What is the plural of mouse? Mause or Mäuse?

What are the "4 cases" of the noun? And how do you recognize them?

After finishing this chapter, you should be able to answer all these questions!

Continue reading...

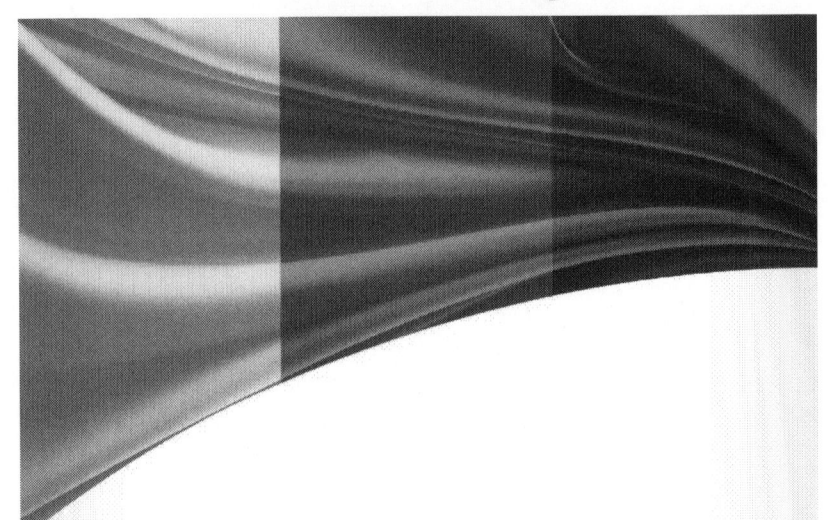

GERMAN

AN ESSENTIAL GUIDE TO GERMAN LANGUAGE LEARNING

LANGUAGE LEARNING UNIVERSITY

Printed in Germany
by Amazon
Distribution